Healing Energies

To Anneliis

May you walk your path in bare feet,
Feeling life's passionate texture,
That's always a treat.
    May you learn your lessons,
From your father's defeats,
And find your own — that would be neat.
    May you look life squarely in the eye,
Knowing you will always fly,
Successfully by.
    Find your passions,
And express them defiantly,
Even against the odds,
Then you will understand,
Life's wonderful desires and
What it's like to dance with the gods.

Healing Energies

UNDERSTANDING AND
USING HANDS-ON HEALING

BRUCE WAY

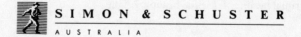

SIMON & SCHUSTER
AUSTRALIA

The information in this book is not intended to be a substitute for medical care and advice. You are advised to consult with your health care professional with regard to all matters relating to your health, including matters which may require diagnosis or medical attention. In particular, if you have any special condition requiring medical attention, or if you are taking, or have been advised to take (or to refrain from taking) any medication, you should consult regularly with your doctor.

All persons referred to in the 'Storyteller' narratives are fictitious and no resemblance to actual persons living or dead should be inferred.

First published in Australia in 2000 by
Simon & Schuster (Australia) Pty Limited
20 Barcoo Street,
East Roseville NSW 2069

A Viacom Company
Sydney New York London Toronto Tokyo
Singapore

National Library of Australia
Cataloguing-in-Publication Data

    Way, Bruce.
    Healing energies: understanding and using
    hands-on healing

    Bibliography

    ISBN 0 7318 0879 7.

    Healing. 2. Healing — Religious aspects. 3.
    Spiritual healing. 4. Mental healing. I. Title.

615.852
Cover photograph: Tony Stone Images,
The Photo Library
Set in Minion 11.25/14.5
Cover design by Gayna Murphy, Greendot Design
Internal design by Vivien Valk,
One Bluedog Design
Printed in Australia by Griffin Press

Contents

Letter to the Reader

I remember I was twelve when my father told my brother and me that Mum had a slight problem. 'Nothing to worry about,' he said. 'She needs an operation, then she will be as good as new.' Little did we know that our mother, Ila, had cancer of the bowel. Dad's philosophy has always been to give everything we do our best shot.

'What happens if you miss?' I sometimes asked him.

'Oh!' He would laugh. 'That's simple. Just try again.' Dad believed that as long as we were breathing there was enough ammunition in life's rifle to take another shot.

Mum had the operation. 'Nothing to worry about,' Dad told us. 'The doctors think that they have taken out all the cancer although they took out more than they wanted to. Mum is quite drained. It will take a while for her to get back onto her feet.' Reality was that my mother was close to death. The surgery was major and she now had a colostomy. That's an opening through the stomach wall connecting the bowel directly to the outside. The surgeons had removed most of her intestines and bowel. A month later she came home. 'Now, that's a positive sign,' Dad declared. 'Once she's in her bed the healing will be quicker.' Time passed and Mum lay in bed with no sign of change. 'Well she's not getting worse,' I overheard Dad say to a concerned friend … and the clock kept ticking.

'We have another development,' Dad announced at breakfast. 'Mum has asked to be anointed.' Anointing is an ancient tradition revered by my parents who were, and still are, devout Christians. Anointing is an Old Testament ritual.

Before the anointing, scheduled to take place in my parent's bedroom, the minister took Brian, my brother, and me aside. 'This is a very sacred event,' he advised. I noted a touch of caution in his voice. My teachers used the same tone to quell mischievous insurrection in the classroom. 'Only people who have confessed *all* their sins to God or man, who hold no anger and carry only love in their hearts can participate in the ceremony.'

I shuddered inwardly, not sure that I could live up to those standards. My mind raced. What about the arguments that I had had with my best friend, John, earlier? I was still mad at him. After all, I was right and he wouldn't admit it.

'If you can't say yes to these conditions then perhaps it's best to stay outside. Your sins could affect your mother's healing,' the minister advised.

Well, I wasn't sure that I had sinned. So perhaps I hadn't. I knew Mum wanted me there and I hoped that was enough. I looked at Brian. He didn't say a word. They ushered us in. The ceremony was short. The minister and selected church elders knelt around Mum. They placed their hands on her head and shoulders. Then prayed, asking God to heal her. I remember feeling guilty because I opened my eyes while they were praying, something that they taught me since birth was wrong. The ritual closed when the minister placed a drop of oil on the top of Mum's head.

'Will it work?' I asked the minister, secretly hoping that my indiscretions hadn't killed her.

'It's in God's hands now,' he replied.

My father cut in quickly, saying, 'We can help by believing that God has healed her'. Everyone paused. Silence fell over the room.

Mum spoke: 'I believe I am healed and that's all that matters'. Two days later Mum was out of bed for the first time since she came home. It was a miracle! In fact, at the time of writing this book, my mother is eighty and still going strong. The operation was thirty-five years ago. That's great for her. It's also great for me because I learnt something. I didn't kill her by opening my eyes or by my less than charitable thoughts about John!

Years passed — about twenty-four of them. I was thirty-six years old, living in Sydney after leaving home at twenty-two. I was single again with a marriage behind me, had left my first religion behind, and developed a fascination for Eastern philosophies. For me, life was about trying to integrate corporate life with an unquenchable thirst for spiritual understanding. Somehow, I enrolled in a Reiki course. Reiki is a Japanese-based hands-on healing system. A Reiki master passes the healing techniques to the student until the student becomes a master and so on. This is how the Reiki fraternity keeps the lineage intact. The master claims to be able to access the universal healing banks and can make us healers, although they keep the actual ritual, and its associated symbols, hidden. This is, supposedly, to protect the system's integrity.

Reiki First Degree is the entry-level course, that usually runs over two days. During the workshop a Reiki master attunes students into the universal healing energy and teaches them how to act as a channel for the energy to others.

As I was rushing to make the second day on time, the telephone rang. 'Hello,' I answered impatiently.

'Hi, honey. What are you doing today?' It was my mother. She always has a knack of ringing when I am exploring some esoteric teaching that I want to keep quiet.

'I'm just on my way out to a hands-on healing course. I can't talk …'

'What's it called?'

'Reiki.'

The line went silent. I could hear Mum deep in thought down the line. 'Oh Bruce!' She finally gathered her thoughts. 'Don't get too close to the devil, son … promise now.'

That's how it started for me. After Reiki First Degree, I developed as a psychic and trance medium. Naturally, a part of my practice was as a spiritual healer. My psychic teachers warned me against Reiki because of the commercial overtones of a system they felt was freely available to everyone. I listened respectfully, then completed Reiki Second Degree. I could find no discernible difference between the Reiki healing system and spiritual healing. Several years passed and I practised part-time as a spiritual healer.

Ironically, the people who sought me out were, in the main, cancer sufferers diagnosed incurable.

Life went on. I wrote my first book *Living Intuitively — Reaping Life's Rich Benefits*, practised as a psychic, worked in the corporate sector, taught psychic development, and ran healing sessions. The Reiki system drifted from my mind. It seemed senseless to put a brand on something generically universal. I finished my second book *Psychic or Charlatan — How to Interpret a Psychic Reading* and then, like many writers, went back to work to earn a living. For me, it was the corporate sector. It was during this time that a friend referred me to Dr Christine Henderson, a senior executive in the Australian banking system.

'I've just got a feeling,' my friend said, 'that you will both benefit from meeting.'

'All I need is more corporate contacts,' I thought. Yet being selfishly money hungry, I rang and made the appointment.

My first meeting with Chris lasted two hours. She spoke of books she had written, her interests in the Kabbalah and in alternate forms of healing. I gave her a psychic reading, spoke of the books I had written and about my spiritual healing practice.

'By the way,' Chris said as we parted, 'I am a Reiki master and a Seichim master.'

I remember walking away thinking, 'So what!'. Yet, her statement haunted me. Later, I rang her and asked if she would attune me into mastership although I could not reason why.

She agreed, saying that because we were friends she would do it for me at a discount. She said that it would take a weekend with a couple of preliminary nights, and that she would personally attune me into Reiki mastery for $3000 and into Seichim mastery for $3500.

I thought I'd slide under the desk in shock. Yet, clutching the telephone as if it were my life raft, I heard myself tell her it was fine. We agreed on the dates and left it at that. I went out for a long lunch to contemplate my rash decision. At that time, I was unaware that Reiki master attunements could cost as much as $U.S20,000.

I kept my date and arrived on time for the Saturday session, planning to dedicate the whole weekend to the attunement process. By lunchtime, Chris had attuned me into Seichim mastery. Seichim (sometimes known as Sekhem), she said, was a system similar to Reiki. A Reiki master, Patrick Zeigler, rediscovered it. It felt great! By 3 pm she had attuned me into Reiki mastery. That felt great too! By 5 pm she had taught me all the symbols and the sequences required to initiate people through all levels into and including the mastery level. I was an accredited Reiki and Seichim master! Moreover, we got there a day early. Now, that presented a quandary. What could we do on the Sunday? As Reiki and Seichim masters, we conferred and decided that there was nothing left to do. Therefore, I had Sunday to integrate the profundity of Saturday's session. I went to the beach with my family.

As the weeks passed, the simplicity of both systems fascinated me, now that I knew the secrets. I could not balance the simplicity with the cost. Nor could I reconcile how intelligent people could wrap simple, wonderful healing energies into a dogmatic ritual based on control. Each time I tried to rationalise the two, my mind took me back to my mum's anointing. Yes, I had opened my eyes. I did resent my friend. I had not confessed my sins and my mother was living proof that these rules just didn't matter. The more I searched for the answers the more my understanding about healing grew.

William Blake, the English poet, artist, and mystic put it this way. He said: 'I must create a system or be enslaved in another man's. I must not reason nor compare, my business is to create'. As my contact with people who doctors had diagnosed as terminally ill increased, Blake's statement also grew in magnitude. Humans are compulsive creators. We can't help it. Try for a moment to think of a day when you did not create something! Humans are creators and in this sense, we are gods! We have an eternal urge to manifest our inner brilliance in an external creative way that is visible in the physical world.

I have written *Healing Energies* from what I have learnt by running two-day workshops called 'Healing with Energies'. These workshops included more than Reiki and Seichim philosophy and practice. They were workshops that explored the magnificence of the human spirit that chooses to find mastery through illness creation, then by health realisation. In *Healing Energies*, I use these two popular hands-on healing traditions as archetypal models to illustrate healing mastery. These models are similar to spiritual healing. At the time of writing *Healing Energies*, more than 4000 people have attended my workshops in Australia, New Zealand, England, Scotland, Ireland and Wales. The feedback I receive always inspires me to encourage others to recognise and express their light in their unique brilliant ways.

In this book, I have outlined the healing attunement sequences and symbols of Reiki and Seichim up to and including the master/teacher levels of both systems that have been kept secret for so long. I believe that it's time to step out from the shadows and demystify a subject where secrecy seems to achieve no spiritual purpose.

I don't expect you to believe what I say, because self-mastery is a journey for you. Masters create their own systems rather than adhere to someone else's. Masters do not need another person to bestow mastery upon them. If you believe that you need another person to bestow mastery upon you, then you haven't reached mastery yet. I find it ironic that people proudly display certificates given to them by another to prove who they are. Surely we are our own certificates. The certificates of others, in my opinion, are merely signs of our feelings of inadequacies. They are statements to the world that we believe that we haven't made it yet. The act of mastery is simply represented by people claiming their birthrights and courageously practising the system that they have created. As a master you are the teacher, you are the student, and, yes, you are the examiner. Therefore, read this book as a catalyst for your growth. As you interact with its concepts and relate intuitively to the subject, you will find new levels of health, wellbeing and creativity.

This book is about physical healing and much more. It is about remembering our wholeness. My thesis is that illness occurs when we move away from expressing our life's mission. The healing process then begins when we realise that we are ill. Therefore, step one in the healing process is illness. The illness then continues as an indicator, beacon or lighthouse, to guide us on the search to find, recognise, and express our life's mission in bringing our daily dreams to fruition. Therefore, step two is in the searching. To find and recognise our mission, we shed outmoded ideas and patterns that block us from seeing who we are. Our illnesses then signal to us when we are at a roadblock along memory lane. Step three in the healing process is when our illness speaks loudly to us and asks us to rest a while and consider who we are.

Illness then is the shadow side of health. Wherever we find the shadow, we know that we have reached the light. The quest of the master's apprentice is to look through the shadows and into that light. It is in this light that our wholeness stands waiting eternally to be recognised, accepted and merged into our conscious being. To live as a master requires remembering who we are and then expressing our wholeness according to the mission we choose to express in the physical world.

Writing this book is a new experience for me. In a sense, it is an anecdotal saga of my journey thus far. No, I haven't been terminally ill. The inspirational case studies of people's journeys with terminal illness are of people who I am privileged to have been touched by. No, I have not reached the greatness that mastery implies. My friends will tell you that I am very much the master's apprentice trying to emulate my dream and creating chaos in my enthusiastic search for self-discovery.

In *Healing Energies*, I have tried to weave different-coloured story threads into the fabric of the text. By anecdote, theory and example I hope to have achieved a holographic story line that will inspire you to take up your bed and walk as you continue to write your story on life's rich tapestry.

Chapter 1

The Storyteller 1

Ted surveyed the apartment that had served as his cocoon for the past thirteen weeks. He laughed as he remembered describing it as a two-storey wardrobe in early dispatches home. Number forty-eight nestled in a wardrobe colony on the eastern wharf at Brighton Marina. It floated on the English tides in synchronous rhythm to the changing international flotilla.

Ready to go, his packed bags stood in a line like obedient soldiers waiting for the command to march. One last time he painstakingly climbed the tight spiral staircase. A staircase resembling elastic steel twisted elegantly to maximise the cramped space.

Ted looked around searching for that forgotten item usually remembered in mid-flight across the Pacific. He saw nothing. He searched the drawers methodically, leaving each drawer open as he moved around the room. Hence, a trail of completion to prevent him wasting time going over ground already trod. Ted paused at the bedside drawer and chuckled. On his arrival he found the drawer filled with condom packets feverishly torn apart. They were torn apart with such fury that Ted could almost hear fingernails breaking in a desire to facilitate climactic passion.

To some the condom represented liberation — or perhaps fornication without a trace. To others, it created the secondary reinforcement. Fear of sex. Fear of passionate spontaneous expression. Fear of creation.

As Ted finished in the loft, he wondered what was the secondary reinforcement that stimulated the fear of his creative expression. During the speaking tour just finished, he had pondered the question obsessively. 'I am a storyteller,' he confessed at the finale of the seminar. A revelation he used to demonstrate his theory about a person's life purpose. 'Find your passion,' he challenged his audiences. 'Have the courage to express your creative brilliance openly and without apology. After all, we are the creators of our realities. And because we are the creators of our realities, we are gods.' The audience usually sat spellbound during the performance.

Ted had the gift. He knew how to engage the audience. He stroked them sensuously, played with them. He could feel when boredom entered the room and instinctively knew when to thrust harder or to lie quietly beside them crooning flattering truths into their openness. 'We are all creators. Just think of a time when you have not created something. Tell me one moment in your conscious state when you haven't created something.' He challenged them with the conviction of authority that defied a negative response. 'And even when you are asleep your body is still creating. New cells replacing the old generate new life. Face it! We just can't help ourselves. We are compulsive creators!'

Then the silence. During the afterglow he would say: 'So what is your life's purpose? Why did you incarnate this time? What part of your divinity did YOU decide to express in YOUR life? It's so simple when you find it. You will just know. That's the purpose of intuition. It's your communicative tool that speaks with your soul. It enables you to find your creative essence and shows you how to express it passionately in your life. And you know it's so simple. That when you find out who you are a knowing will just click into your heart and you will find peace.'

The seminar finished. Silence. The audience had travelled with him for two days. Insight dawned on each person at different times. Ted was the orator, the master, the author, and the expert. They came to sit with him, to benefit from his wisdom. He could lead them to the Holy Grail. Show them the way. Yet at the climax, the crescendo of his performance, the message was always the same. 'Only you know who you are. No-one can tell you. It's up to you to find out who you are. I know you can do it because I know you are divine.' Then his opening words fell into context and the audience understood.

'At the outset of the course there are two conditions. The first is not to believe anything I say because it may not be relevant to you. Just use my words as a catalyst and observe the responses they generate within you. One truth that I have learnt is that the more knowledge I acquire, the less I can say that it's absolutely right. Learning is a continuum. My truth today could quite possibly be different to what I believe a year from now. We live and grow in a developmental world. We learn by experience. We learn by interacting with our environment. We learn by discussion. We learn by debate. We learn by watching television. We learn by our mistakes. Life is about learning from experience. Learning stops when you have had enough of the experience. Then you look back and realise why the experience happened.'

Ted believed strongly that New Agers promoted living in the present moment at the expense of past experience. He felt that it was erroneous to believe that the past holds us back. The value of the past, according to Ted, was that it gives people the history to look back and say, 'What are we going to learn from this?'. On one hand we say we live in the moment. In the moment life is static. Yet, at the same time we develop a flow. 'Life, paradoxically, is a static continuum.' Ted usually grinned when he spat that one out.

He would tell his audience: 'The first commitment is that you don't believe anything I say. If you believe my words then you are going to stop thinking about what I am saying. I'm purely the catalyst. I'm here as the person who's going to relate my experiences to what I believe to be the truth. I'll give you honest Ted Ryan because that's all I can do but that doesn't mean that I am right. Who knows what percentage of right I am? And what is right for me may be absolutely wrong for you. It's your choice. Everything is your choice.

'Put that into the healing modality for a moment. If a person comes to me with a terminal illness, do I tell them what I think they need to do to heal? Or am I going to say, "It's your life, you have the power to heal yourself". The instant I set myself up as a guru or as a miracle healer, neon lights flash. "Ego talking!" If people believe that I can do it for them, then the power will shift from their healing self to me. Well, I don't want that. If I did, then perhaps my ego is feeling frail and looking for an image boost.

'Test everything I say with your inner sense. Test it with your intuition and decide for yourself. Yet never be afraid to change your mind. Remember the key to healing is to develop on the static continuum. The more I work in the healing area, the more I realise that I know nothing about it. The more I see people heal from so-called incurable situations, the more I realise just how incredible the human spirit is. So why suppress it with dogma, ritual, beliefs and conditions etched in stone? This weekend I will talk about people with terminal illnesses because they are the most empowered people I've witnessed. Why? Because the system has cut them free by simply saying that it can't help them. They are on their own paths taking responsibility for their unique destinies and they are doing it without the curse of the compassionate — hope. When there is no hope there is a simple decision to make. Either to take up their beds and walk or to remain dependant on the powerless.

'Over the next two days we will discuss the ethics of healing and how to be an effective healer. We will define illness and realise that it is only one way to describe imbalance. Therefore, healing applies to more than the physical or emotional conditions. Healing energy can touch any facet of life that is out of balance and holds our lives in balance once we get there. Therefore, healing energy is relevant to a company heading towards bankruptcy, a relationship in conflict and a writer with writer's block.

'Healing is purely the practice of bringing the unbalanced situation into alignment. Usually that requires creative and innovative talents. Talents that people demonstrate continuously by forever creating their realities. The healing process helps people realise their creative brilliance. Now, that's exciting!

'I am going to talk about God today and tomorrow. I'm not a religious person. When I talk about spiritual things I am not talking about theology. I am not talking about religion. I'm talking about a characteristic of the essence that we can't physically relate to that we call spirit. If we look at the general definition of God, then the nature of God knows no limitations and is eternally creative. Every day we observe people showing this God characteristic because they are continually creating something new out of nothing. We create as a reflex action. It is just a reflex action because of who we are.

'Think for a moment how society actually sets itself up to disprove what I've just said.'

'Excuse me,' comes a faint voice from the back row. 'You're talking about conditions that we have to agree upon. You've only told us one.'

Ted grimaced. He had the tendency to shoot off on tangents. He saw it as a flaw in his character. 'Sorry.' He apologised, genuinely embarrassed, and continued.

'The second condition is that for the duration of our time together you accept the notion that you are absolutely responsible for everything that happens in your life. Oh … and there is a third condition. Sorry, because I don't believe in conditions. The third condition is that you don't have to accept the first two conditions.'

The workshop finished. The queue for book signings formed. Ted graciously received all autograph hunters and wrote a personal note in each book. He was always the salesman. He smiled at the people who asked, 'Do you mind signing my book?'. 'God, no. Any author lives for this moment. I could do this all day for nothing.' Eventually the line dwindled and the audience drifted back to their lives leaving Ted alone.

On the way to his room, the euphoric stage energy fell away, leaving a void within him so great that he wondered if these mood swings meant he was a manic-depressive. Once in his room, he flicked on the television, scanned for something of interest, opened the mini-bar and wondered why people listened to him. Sure, he had two books published but he had written nothing new for at least three years — well, not anything serious. There was the odd poem and his first stage play was unproduced, waiting to mate with a suitable theatre company. 'I am the storyteller. So why don't I write!' he yelled.

A sharp knock on the door jolted Ted. He looked around the wardrobe's mezzanine to regain his bearings. The knock came again. Ted scurried down the stairs.

Chapter 2
Soulful Healing

Many years ago, I began practising as a spiritual healer. People came to me with their aches and pains. I laid my hands on them. Sometimes they left feeling better and sometimes the cure seemed permanent. During the sessions, I thought I could sense something happening, though I was never sure. I am my own biggest skeptic and like many healers I vacillate from a position of 'This stuff is really powerful' to a position of 'How do I know if what I am doing really works? Perhaps the person just thought themselves back to health'.

My first contact as a hands-on healer happened quickly after I qualified as a Reiki First Degree practitioner. To qualify as a Reiki One I needed to undertake a two-day workshop. There were no prerequisites to enter the course. Jerry, the Reiki master, on giving us our certificates, declared that we, his students of two days, were now capable of healing others. We could do this, he declared, because he had *attuned* us through four separate attunements that weekend into the Reiki energy. 'Imagine that you are like a water hose'. He said. 'What I do by attuning you is to connect you to the tap and turn it on for you. After that, the flow is automatic. It will turn itself on or off whenever you want to give healing and place your hands within two inches of the person.' Reiki, he said, was the finest vibrational healing energy of the universe. It was the energy of the river of life and by tapping into it we could share the river with as many people as desired it.

What he said seemed reasonable to me. After all, Jerry was an accredited Reiki master and had the certificates to prove it. Before I enrolled in the workshop, I wanted to be a healer yet did not believe that I could do it. Having completed Reiki One, I had my certificate and the endorsement of a master. Therefore, whenever I doubted my ability, I could look at the certificate and know that someone believed that I had the gift. Practice, he said, was the best way to increase this newly discovered talent.

'Just imagine that your garden hose has been lying out in the weather unused for a year. It will be stiff and inflexible. As you let the water flow through your hose, it will become more flexible and will expand so that more water can pass through. Therefore, the more people you can practise on, the better.' These were his final words of encouragement. My problem was that I didn't know anyone who was sick, at least well enough to practise on them.

My parents raised me as a Christian, carrying the brand name of Seventh-Day Adventist. They taught me to ask God for whatever I wanted. Although, as an adult, I had moved on from their faith, the training was bred into me. As a child, I prayed to God and asked for the most fantastic things to happen. Sometimes they did. Now as an adult, I had put away childish things and had found the New Age. Therefore, instead of God I now commanded the universe to provide the miraculous. Well, what's in a name anyway? After Jerry's edict, I put it out to the universe for someone to practise on. Much to my surprise, the universe, disguised as a friend, rang me.

'Bruce,' he said. 'I hear you've just finished Reiki First Degree. Do you want some practice?' Alan had a friend who had severe spinal problems after falling from a horse. The situation was so serious that the doctors had scheduled Thomas, his friend, for surgery to fuse three spinal disks. 'He's got nothing to lose,' Alan encouraged me. 'Tom is desperate. He will try anything. So you may as well have a crack at him.' After such encouragement, I could hardly refuse.

I visited Tom shortly after. His wife greeted me at the door because Tom was unable to walk up or down the three flights of stairs that meandered between floors of their inner city terrace. I climbed the three flights to Tom's bedroom. He lay on his back, prostrate, on the bed.

'I hope you can fix this,' he said in desperation. 'If you can't then I have to be operated on.' I looked at him hesitantly. 'Well, can you?' he asked.

'I don't know,' I replied. 'You are my first client.' With that resounding statement of confidence, I helped him roll onto his stomach and placed my hands up and down his spine for an hour and a half. At times, I felt incredible heat, at other times I felt cold. For most of the time, I felt nothing at all. Yet, despite believing that the healing wasn't working, Thomas kept commenting that he felt relief from the pain.

Sometime during the session, Tom and I had bonded, in a male sort of way. We became deeply engrossed in a discussion about Chinese philosophy. I finished the healing. He rolled onto his back. We kept talking. Tom sat up and swung his feet onto the floor. Still deep in conversation we descended the stairs. Still talking, he walked me to the door.

'Thomas! What are you doing out of bed?' his wife exclaimed. Tom and I stared blankly at each other, not realising what had happened.

'I guess I forgot,' Thomas weakly apologised. 'My back feels free and there is no pain.' I looked at him in amazement.

'I hope it lasts,' I said and left. Driving home, I remember thinking that the chances were that no healing took place. Probably he just relaxed with the human contact, I thought.

Two years passed by. 'You won't remember me,' the stranger said. 'I'm Thomas. You worked on me several years ago. I don't know what you did but when I was x-rayed the next day there was no sign of a problem. I never had the operation! I have always wondered what you did,' he said.

I stared at him blankly, trying to think of an answer. 'Actually, Tom, I haven't a clue what happened,' I reassured him.

'Well, it has all of us baffled,' he said.

'All of us?' I asked.

'Yes, my colleagues and myself.'

I asked Thomas what he and his colleagues did.

'Didn't you know? We are surgeons in the spinal unit.'

That's right! The person who had asked for the healing was a specialist surgeon in the spinal unit of a recognised teaching hospital.

The chances are that you will be reading this book for one of four reasons. Perhaps you have contracted an illness that has been difficult to shake off, keeps recurring, diagnosed as incurable, or is terminal. You may suspect that you are a healer and want to increase your ability to heal those who need it. Perhaps you have a friend or relative that you want to help. Or perhaps you just want free Reiki and Seichim attunements. Whatever your reason for reading this book, you have an interest in healing. The action following your intention is the turning of the pages and your reading of them. Can you hold that thought in the recesses of your mind? It will make sense further into the text.

The notions of healing and our perspectives on it are varied. We have traditionally wrapped healing up in religious dogma, philosophical debate about the nature of life and scientific research and application. Yet, no matter how hard we try to form consistent laws about health and wellbeing the exceptions always pop up like daffodils in the springtime. For example, my great-grandfather, by all reports, was a proud Scotsman. He enjoyed a good dram o' whisky, smoked cigars profusely, and lived a healthy life well into his nineties. Yet others with the same lifestyle suffer from the medically predicted diseases associated with alcohol and tobacco intake. Why do some people heal and some people do not? What is the definition of healing? Is there a universal panacea or …? There are just so many unanswered questions.

I believe that the exceptions to the rule are indeed the daffodils in our gardens. They lie dormant, well hidden in the ground, until they sense the subtle energy shift in the seasons. Then an urge manifests to send a shoot upward to find the open air where each bulb can express its brilliance. Horticulturists have a wonderful word to describe the germination process. They call it 'perturbation'.

Perturbation occurs when the bulb (or seed) undergoes tremendous pressure that motivates the seed to shoot. Illness, and hence the healing process, in my opinion, is the perturbation process of the seed that contains our creative brilliance. Illness, then, is a process that brings to our attention the possibility that, planted within our soul's garden, is a potential so great that we keep it buried because it will take a huge shift in consciousness to accept it.

I suggest that we base our definitions of healing on our particular philosophical, theological and theosophical beliefs about the nature of life. As such, *Healing Energies* is a subjective discussion about the metaphysics of health. I draw on personal experience and observation to write this work. I am uninterested in scientific-based medical research. Not because I believe it to be without value; rather, my contention is that we base everything we do on personal beliefs about the purpose and function of the universe. The basis for this discussion assumes that we are infinite divine beings who are compulsive-obsessive creators. I have no interest in proving my assertions or in providing at length reasons for healings or non-healings. In my mind, such discussion is purely a rationalisation of a simple intrinsic truth. We are the divine creators of our reality. That ill health is no more or less than a state of being out of balance with the soul's desires to creatively express itself in the physical world.

I always open each 'Healing with Energies' workshop by asking the audience not to believe what I say. Sounds crazy, yet it is true. I am running a workshop about how to heal people and I am asking them to discount what I am teaching! A human reflex is to create belief systems that convince us that we can function safely in the environment around us. It is the role of the ego to keep us safe. In order to keep us safe the ego must first believe that we are unsafe or at least that there is a possibility of danger. Therefore, it tests the world on our behalf to formulate rules and conditions that we could call our modus operandi. When we operate within this modus operandi, we assume that we are safe.

In *Living Intuitively*, I use the following to define fear as a belief in 'False Expectations Appearing Real'. Not all fears eventuate, as we saw from my account of opening my eyes at my mother's prayer session. When we act from ego, we function in such a way as to avoid feared outcomes. Therefore, we try to control or manipulate our environment. Let's take a person, Jealous John, as an example. John is jealous because he fears that his girlfriend will be disloyal to him. Although there is no evidence to suggest this, John modifies his behaviour to avoid the feared outcome. That is the pain resulting from rejection. What can John do to avoid the feared pain? He might decide to socialise only with his girlfriend to keep the baying male competition away. At parties, he may never leave his girlfriend's side. He may act more subtly and try to evoke a sense of guilt in his girlfriend so that she will only spend time with him. Whichever way he behaves, John is trying to manipulate and control his environment and another person to avoid facing his fear of rejection.

Alternatively, John could decide to face his fear and discover the truth. Either that his girlfriend is loyal or that she isn't and the pain of rejection is easier to take than the mental effort of manipulating every meeting. If it is the latter, then by avoiding the fear, John has lost an opportunity to heal a part of his personality: a belief that he is not acceptable in his own right. This simple example shows that John's fear can be a positive signpost directing him to a part of his personality that is out of balance with his soul state of perfection. I suggest that whenever we establish rules or modus operandi that become law, we inhibit our growth and this is self-defeating rather than creative. Yet, as we will discover later in the text, even the ego cannot keep us from our divine destiny. It just takes a little longer to get there if we follow our fears.

If the ego establishes belief systems, then as we move and explore our environments we learn to overcome our fears, and our rules about life — our beliefs — change. I remember driving a taxicab on the night shift. It was 2 am in Sydney on a weeknight and there were no cars in sight. As I drove through the city I stopped at a red light, and waited and waited. The rule is that if I cross through a red light, I will have an accident or the police will fine me. Neither possibility appealed to me so I just sat there. It soon became apparent that the lights were jammed and I had to make a decision either to turn the car around to find another way through the city or challenge my belief system and drive through the red light. I decided to risk it and drove through the intersection. That is, I confronted a belief system and neither of the anticipated fears happened. Therefore, I modified my belief about red lights.

Note the difference here between a stated law and strong advice. The stated law about red lights says that if we drive through them we will be hurt in some way. That is, there is no room for movement. This is the karmic model or the law of cause and effect model. Religions of all creeds have built-in laws to modify and change our behaviours. Usually they revolve around doing wrong (sinning) and the consequences of breaking the law. In Christian teaching, a much-quoted passage in the Bible is, 'The wages of sin is death'. Therefore, we affirm a direct link between breaking a law and some kind of loss of something desirable. Here, 'the wages of sin is death' is not very subtle in explaining to us that if we sin then we won't receive eternal life.

Notice the conditions here. The link words in any conditional statement are IF and THEN. IF we sin THEN we will lose our life. The ego then works from a position where it motivates the personality to avoid loss. Now if you are very clever you will soon learn that if you can convince people that they will lose something that they value then you can motivate them to behave in ways that you want them to act.

Let's move away from religious connotations and apply this theory to daily life. Meet James, a successful businessman. He is married with two beautiful children, lives in an affluent suburb in the home of his dreams surrounded by all the possessions he has ever wanted. To acquire these things he has taken a mortgage on his home, leased the cars and borrowed enough to pay for his children's education at the best schools. James can do this because he is a chartered accountant with a major accounting practice and has the income to support the loans. Joyce, his wife, on the other hand is not that happy. She feels left out and unfulfilled. Her artistic career stopped when she had the children, and although she loves them deeply, she now wants to go back to work in the profession she loves. Yet every time she talks with James he tells her that it is not possible for her to re-enter the workforce because being a stripper in a nightclub is not considered a suitable occupation by his employer.

How they resolve their dilemma would make a great stage play. Notice how this simple scenario soon becomes complicated when we apply the IF/THEN 'Model of Loss' to their plight. James could well say, 'Joyce, I love you dearly. Yes, I know we met at the strip joint and I just love your work but —'. Let's stop the stage play here. Another word has crept silently and unobtrusively into the dialogue. The 'but' word. Always be aware of the 'but' word because it usually is the word that forewarns the IF/THEN plot. Let's go back to the script.

ACT ONE, SCENE THREE:

JAMES: Joyce, I love you dearly. Yes I know we met at the strip joint and I just love your work but you know that the firm takes its clients to that club. If someone recognises you then I could lose my job.

JOYCE: What would be so bad about that? I don't see you anyway. You are always working. James, the firm really uses you.

JAMES: You don't understand. If I lose my job then I can't keep up the payments on the house, the car or the school fees. We would probably have to sell the antiques to pay for the kids' education. Can't you just wait until we own everything? Then we can take some risks.

In the play, Joyce decides to sacrifice her creative expression for a while longer until they reduce the risk of loss.

Ten years pass. James is now the managing partner for the Pacific Basin. They own their home, their cars, have no debt and they have enough saved for the rest of the school fees. One day James comes home excited ...

JAMES: I have great news. The biggest chartered firm in the world has approached me. They want us to sell up and move to Chicago. Honey, this is the job I have always dreamed of.

JOYCE: That's great, darling. What's the nightclub scene like there? No-one will know me, so I can resume my career.

JAMES: Um, I don't think it would be appropriate, precious. I can't have even the whisper of anything like that. Most of our clients will be senior politicians.

JOYCE: (*Loses it*) Well, James, that's it. If I can't work as a stripper over there, then I am not going. I will leave you.

JAMES: But Joyce, you can't leave me. A condition of the job is that I have a wife to entertain clients. If you don't come with me, then I can't take the job.

The scene ends with Joyce acquiescing to James' career aspirations and suppressing her own creative expression. Life continues for another ten years. James' career builds, until he becomes the first Australian adviser to the President of the United States of America. Joyce, on the other hand, gets lung cancer, which the doctors advise is terminal. They give her three months to live. The shock of losing her motivates James to give up his career and devote his time exclusively to Joyce. She has one wish granted, as is common with patients who are terminally ill, and becomes the world's oldest stripper. She is so happy now that she is finally expressing her creativity that she forgets she has cancer and loses track of time. The three months pass and the results of her tests show that the tumour has shrunk. The doctors now increase her life expectancy to two years.

Sorry. My enthusiasm carried me away, or did it? The karmic model operates throughout every part of our lives. People control other people every second of the day by suggesting the possibility of loss and trading off the resultant fear. They do this by establishing belief systems that state categorically that if I do something then I will lose something. Let's go back to the red traffic light example. Rules and laws do have a place in society. The purpose of developing a standard system of coloured traffic lights is to allow cohesive traffic flow. That's valid. The debilitating effects of laws occur when they transmute from guidelines to unchangeable fact. We can state the traffic light rule in a more empowering way: by advising people that when the traffic light is red there is a distinct possibility that cars will be travelling on the crossroad and that it is dangerous to cross. Therefore, the advice would be to stop at the red light until the person has ascertained that it is safe to proceed.

To operate from our ego responses of fear and loss, I suggest, inhibits our creative expression. I believe that our creative expression is the manifestation in the physical world of soulful desire. Therefore, to suppress such expressive desires creates an imbalance between our spiritual natures and our physical natures.

I also believe that the soul is the divine or god part of our being. As such, it breathes life into our physical natures. I define physical to encompass our behaviour, emotions and thoughts as well as flesh and blood. Therefore, the more disassociated our physical natures become from our spiritual selves, the more the physical becomes starved from the soul's life-giving energies. Hence, illness to me is evidence of the degree of separation of the personality from the soul. Healing then takes place when the soul has an unobstructed avenue to create its bliss in the physical world.

When the soul speaks the spirit moves and the person creates. When the soul speaks, the spirit moves and the personality hesitates and listens to the ego's fears. Then imbalances occur. Our creations take on inappropriate manifestations. These shadow creations manifest as illness in the physical realm. We become unbalanced, dissatisfied, and de-motivated while our lives take on a persona less than divine. It's then that the ancient Sufi saying points us back into the realm of wellness and the process of healing is activated. 'Our deepest fear is not that we are inadequate. Our deepest fear is that we are powerful beyond measure. It is our light, not our darkness, that most frightens us.'

Chapter 3

The Storyteller 2

'Well, everything packed?' Pete asked as he squeezed his way inside. Then he looked at his watch. 'We've got plenty of time. Your flight leaves Heathrow at two, doesn't it?' Ted grunted confirmation. 'We should be right even if the motorways are jammed. Plenty of time,' Pete continued as if he needed reassurance. The two stood in the narrow hallway looking at each other. Simultaneously, Pete and Ted fell into a silent hole which neither wanted to emerge from and face the reality of the moment. For a season, they had travelled the same path, faced the same challenges, theorised ad nauseum, and speculated endlessly. Both had put their financial security on the line for this tour. They thought it couldn't fail. The market demographics agreed, every psychic, astrologer and seer that they sought advice from had confirmed the success of the venture.

Pete loaded himself with luggage and left the rest for Ted. They travelled in silence, their thoughts unspoken. Inside, Ted was a backwash of emotions. Grief, relief, anticipation, regret, frustration, feelings of failure and perhaps guilt at the possibility of being a fraud, all eroded his soul.

Thirteen weeks prior he sat on QF 001 leaving Sydney for London, in business class, full of hope. He had quit his job as CEO of an Australian software house to embark upon a life of his creation. 'It will be fine, Marianne,' he reassured his partner. 'It's only thirteen weeks and I will make more money in that time than in a normal year. With the exchange rate at three dollars to the pound, it just spells success.' This was Ted's dream. To live the life his soul cried out to experience. Now he was twenty hours away from his reunion with her and he had to tell her that all he had to show for his work was three hundred quid. He had no work lined up in Oz and a pile of debts stacked higher than their house. Instead of the 2000-strong audiences cumulated across twelve venues they had budgeted for, only 120 had sold. While that paid for the tour cost, it didn't recoup the $160,000 invested by his partner and himself.

'Ted,' Pete broke the silence. 'We are here. Let's check you in. We have time for a cappuccino. I think we can afford that,' Pete chuckled nervously. Ted thought of the irony as his bags disappeared along the conveyor belt.

'The cost of the ticket is more than the money we made,' he whined to Pete.

'Bollocks!' Pete snapped.

'I just don't understand it. Everyone we consulted said it would work. Even our critics agreed. I have never had a more unanimous response,' Ted continued.

'C'mon Ted, we've been over this before. It did work. You were accepted. You got your foot in the door of a new country. Look at the letters of thanks that came in after each seminar. You did a great job.' Pete tried to soak up his cappuccino with sugar.

'Yeah! One hundred and one thousand flyers, Pete, sent right into the target market. One hundred and twenty-six people. We didn't even make a marketer's fail rate.

'Ted, let it go. It's done. We'll be back next year. We have a client base now. Every person you spoke to wants to hear you again. Our estimate is that if each person brings a …'

'And how can we afford the airfares?' Ted felt his anger rise. 'I'm not swimming over here. I just can't understand it. God! I teach prosperity and look …' What he wanted to say, but lacked the courage to, was that he had been on this merry-go-round for most of his adult life. Sure, there had been respites but just when the balance came, he would try something new and gamble everything he had on it and lose — financially at least.

Those who heard him talk or read his books sung his praises. No-one doubted his sincerity or integrity. Except Ted.

'And then there was the time,' he confided to an audience, 'when I was going through one of my financial low points. I have them every so often. About once a day.' The audience laughed. 'I remember talking at a 'Mind, Body, Spirit Festival' in Sydney. The topic was 'Living Intuitively — Reaping Life's Rich Benefits'. There were about 100 people in the audience.' Numbers were always important to Ted. They verified his worth somehow. 'I had enough money for my bus fare home and there I was talking about prosperity. As I left the convention centre, a man came up to me.

'"Excuse me Ted," he said. "I just want to thank you. I came to your talk two years ago. At the time, I was facing bankruptcy. I had to find $30,000 in two days or I was gone. After your talk, I applied what you said and it worked. I created the money and never went bankrupt." The man shook my hand with such gratitude. And all I wanted to do was ask him how he did it!' The audience roared with approval.

A lady shouted. 'Well, did you … ask him, I mean?'

Ted shook his head. 'I didn't want to break his bubble.' There was the lie. What ego! Ted was the master/teacher who knew in his heart that the reason that he chose not to ask the question was that he lacked the humility to be real.

'At least you are flying home business class.' Pete pulled Ted back into reality.

Ted laughed. 'Don't have to pay for the drinks. Rich in frequent flyers and … well, it seems it's all about image. Look good on the outside.' Then he said, 'Why do I feel so hollow inside? I feel so sick.'

Pete grabbed Ted by the shoulders in a firm brotherly way and said: 'Unless you stop feeling sorry for yourself, I will belt some sense into that thick skull of yours. Ted, shut up and get on the plane! Give the whole thing a month to settle down and when we're back in Oz then it will be time for the appraisals.' They silently walked to the exit and embraced each other gratefully.

'Thanks for travelling with me on this. I'm only sorry that it hasn't worked out the way we hoped. See you back in Oz.' He turned and walked to the gate.

'Ted?' Pete called after him. Ted turned and looked back. 'Just remember. The master always teaches from a kit bag of mistakes.' With that, Pete disappeared into the terminal.

Ted took a deep breath to hold back the tears, reached for his passport and walked to the departure gate.

'On your way home?' the official asked. Ted nodded. 'Taking any duty free with you?' the woman in blue continued.

'Not this time,' Ted replied. 'Only a kit bag of mistakes.'

Chapter 4

Mastery: the Myth of the Meek

Mastery. What a word! We see it touted in advertising. It is the credential of credentials. In sporting events, we have the masters championships. We talk about people respectfully as masters of their fields. In New Age groups, we hear of the ascended masters. I've sometimes joked that the ascended masters are indeed the people to follow because they, at least, had enough sense to escape this reality! Seriously, though, in the healing modalities we hear of the healing masters. One modern-day master was a Japanese gentleman by the name of Dr Mikao Usui. Disciples of Dr Usui claim that he was the founder and master healer of the Reiki system of hands-on healing. In a later chapter, we will be studying the Reiki system in depth. Dr Usui was from the Eastern tradition of masters.

To call a person a master denotes that person as someone who is experienced in something and worthy to teach it. The Reiki and Seichim systems put a lot of emphasis on masters/teachers. These people have the wisdom to apply the healing energy masterfully. The Reiki and Seichim hierarchies authorise their masters to teach the healing secrets to those they deem as ready and suitable.

Now, although I will take several shots at the hierarchies of these systems, I need to make one thing clear. The healing energies work, and have nothing to do with the political and commercial overtones of the organisational structures. By reading this book, you will gain a better understanding of both systems, including all of the secret symbols and sequences that masters use to attune people. By examining the systems of Reiki and Seichim, I hope to show you that healing is a natural reflex of the human spirit and that in our attempts to deify it we have actually rendered the energies impotent.

Similarly, we can use these two healing models as metaphors for life. Indeed, when we extract the principles of manipulation and control from these systems and apply them in general terms to the world, as we know it, we gain greater conscious understanding of the linear world of impermanence. We call this world 'karmic' and it functions on the premise stated in the law of cause and effect. It is a world in which the masters travel over the centuries to show us that we can also become masters of our lives by simply taking up our beds and walking.

Let's then look at three world-recognised masters — Jesus, the Nazarene, Mother Teresa and the Buddha — and examine just what makes them tick. I was raised an orthodox Christian and the stories of Jesus still sit fondly in my heart. Miracles permeate the reports of Jesus' time on earth. He turned water into wine, walked on water, healed the sick and fed 5000 people with the equivalent of a McDonald's Big Mac Meal. Jesus' life was one of demonstrating miracles. We use miracles, then, as a way of proving the divine nature of the miracle performer. It is the miracle or overt divine expression into the physical world that, to some, denotes a master.

A particular story about the Nazarene always touches me. It is the account of Jesus healing the crippled man. The reported story tells of a crowd so thick around the Nazarene that it was impossible for the crippled man's friends to get the man's stretcher close to him. Being innovative human beings, they didn't give up and go home. They didn't take a number and wait for it to be called. Rather, they went up onto the roof, tore a hole in it, and lowered the man on his stretcher down through the opening on ropes. Imagine the scene in today's setting. We have a notable healer talking to the masses when plaster, splinters of wood, and incredible noise falls over the audience. Then, through the ceiling, we see a man suspended on ropes. Jesus stopped his talk and looked at the crippled man. 'Take up your bed and walk,' Jesus commanded. The man stood up. Then picked up his bed and left. The audience who witnessed this event cried miracle and Jesus' status took on new dimensions for all who heard the story.

Miracles impress people. This one was no exception. Now here come the foibles of human nature. The man walked and humanity praised the person who made the suggestion! Think about that for a moment. How did Jesus do it? How did he make the crippled man walk? The answer is difficult to find because there is no physical rationale that sits comfortably with our philosophies and scientific theory. Because we don't have an answer we simply assume that he is God and that he can do it. Miracles traditionally have been the domain of the gods. We are humans, therefore we are not gods. We are taught to believe that miracles are out of our reach. That is, we deify events and the people associated with them when we cannot understand the mechanics of that event.

Deepak Chopra, in a lecture I attended, told us that 'the only difference between sick people and well people is that sick people *have forgotten the memory that they are whole.*' In six hours of superb oratory, this statement stands out for me. 'The only difference between sick people and well people is *that sick people have forgotten the memory that they are whole.*' Wow! Now, there is a revelation. How does our reality change if we assume that we are whole and we have just forgotten that we are? Notice even as I write this, I have difficulty in stating that we are whole definitely. Let's drop the word 'assume' and replace it with 'know'. What happens to our world when we know that we are whole? What happens to our fears when we know that we are safe? What happens to our courage when we know who we are? If we answer these questions honestly then the conclusions are staggering.

The Nazarene said to the cripple, 'Take up your bed and walk'. Let's put this into a modern-day setting. Imagine if Jesus was a regular New Age sort of guy. He is a Reiki and Seichim Master, has studied rebirthing, naturopathy, gestalt counselling and reads all the latest books on the subject. He is at the Royal Albert Hall in London talking to a capacity house on healing when a man moves down the aisle in his motorised wheelchair and asks to be healed.

Jesus looks at the man, feels his sincerity and says: 'Having just done a psychic scan, I can tell you that the problem is in your left knee. You must have issues with your mother that need releasing. I think the trauma relates to when you were three-and-a-half years of age. Let's see. If you want to be healed then I suggest ten weeks of regression therapy.'

Can you hear the conditional nature of the healing?

Jesus says, 'Rebirthing is suitable for that. We need to replace the restriction with flow so let's strap a rose quartz crystal to it ...'

Perhaps if the Nazarene was a medical doctor, he would say: 'A lot can be done with a knee reconstruction these days. We can use keyhole surgery to minimise the scarring. If that fails, we can amputate. Prostheses are all the rage and come in a very appealing range of colours ...'

Jesus said nothing of the sort. He simply said to the man, 'Take up your bed and walk'. Perhaps he saw something in the man that others had missed. Now let's get radical. Perhaps Jesus didn't see the person as sick at all. Perhaps he looked at the crippled man and remembered that he was whole, then he spoke to the man in such a way that ignited the man's memory that he was whole. Perhaps it is as simple as that. Perhaps a quality of mastery that Jesus displayed was the ability to convey truth to others in a way that they would hear it. Perhaps, as a master, Jesus was disciplined to recognise truth and not be distracted by the illusion of illness. The crippled state was merely a distortion in the ability of the man to understand the reality that he was whole.

Consider that we are the creators of our existence. That everything that happens to or in our lives is a manifestation of our focused intention — whether consciously or unconsciously — and what we focus on we create. To illustrate, imagine driving along a highway at night. You have been driving for several hours and are tired. You look along the road and notice that, in the distance, a large truck with its headlights on high beam is coming towards you. You know that the closer you get to the truck the greater the danger of hitting it. You tell yourself that you must not collide with the truck. You also decide that in order to stay safe you must keep it in your sight at all times. You therefore focus directly into the headlights of the oncoming vehicle. Now an interesting thing happens as you get close to the truck. The more you look into the lights the more your car drifts across the road until you are now driving directly towards your own accident. What we focus on we are drawn towards. What we are drawn towards we create.

The way we safely pass the truck is to acknowledge its presence and then ignore it. Sure, we know where the danger lies. Yet instead of focusing on the danger we focus our intention on where we want to go. Therefore, as we draw close to the oncoming truck we look through the glare of its headlights and into the darkness. Then, when we reach the truck, we cannot see anything. The lights blind us. All we can do is hold on to our memory of the road ahead and keep going. Now, imagine driving with a passenger.

While the truck is approaching, the passenger tells you every minute or so: 'Better keep an eye on that truck. Don't forget where the truck is. I am glad that you are driving. I couldn't concentrate with those lights shining in my eyes. You are such a good driver, I really feel safe with you'. Although the passenger is giving you support, they are also directing your attention to the situation that you want to avoid.

In life we face this truck every day. It becomes the phantom menace. For example, suppose a person comes to you with chronic headaches. Do we ask: 'How are the headaches today? I just want you to know that I support you in your condition and sympathise with you. I really feel for you and your problem'. Compassion is an insidious reinforcement of the condition the person wants to forget. The person with the headaches has come to the healer to be relieved of the condition and the healer refocuses them back into the space that they want to leave.

I remember a few years back when I was a struggling author. My friends were really concerned for my wellbeing. They telephoned me regularly to ask about my progress. Usually I moaned to them about my problems. It felt good to get the problems off my chest and out into the open. My friends sympathised with my plight. They told me how much they felt for me and so on. This became a regular part of my life and I really appreciated having such good friends.

Until one day Katrina, my partner, said, 'Bruce, I have been listening to you complaining to our friends for months. Have you ever thought about the time that you waste focusing on your problems? Just consider what more you could achieve if you did something productive in that time.'

Katrina's subtle Aries manner fell on my Virgoan head with the gentleness of a rock crusher at a demolition site. Alas, she was right. My well-meaning friends were focusing me on the truck!

I have another friend, Neil. He is a great buddy. I can always rely on him and he certainly has a great shoulder to cry on. If I feel down, I can call him. However, when I start talking about the truck, Neil will usually intervene. 'Bruce, I haven't got time to listen to your problems. You will get through them. You always do. I see you achieving all the time. When have you got time for a game of golf?'

Take up your bed and walk. What an empowering statement! The Nazarene gave us a clue to mastery. That is masters know who they are and more importantly they know who we are. The master has remembered that we are whole, whereas the initiate is still trying to find the memory. Karmic travellers and religious devotees are yet to entertain the slightest possibility of wholeness. They rely on people to do it for them. They need masters.

In days past I had a small healing practice where I saw only those whom the medical professions labelled terminally ill. The only agreement that we ever made was not to talk about their conditions. I firmly believe that the role of a healer is to encourage clients to see their own brilliance and acknowledge that we are the perfect creators of our reality. In a sense, a healing master is the driving instructor. The client is the learner driver. Then, every time the passenger asks, 'What do I do about that truck up ahead?' the driver says: 'No problem. Just focus on the clear road past the truck'. In a later chapter I will describe the journeys of four of these drivers and explore in detail the nature of illness.

Mother Teresa is another master. I remember being told about a group of people who had obtained an audience with her. They looked forward with excitement to this event and they travelled halfway around the world for their destined meeting. When they arrived at the meeting place they were ushered into a small room with a table and six chairs in the centre. They noticed that this was odd, as there were six of them. They wondered where Mother Teresa would sit. At the other end of the room was another door with a tapestry screen placed in front of it. The group spoke amongst themselves as they waited. They discussed who would speak first, what type of questions they would ask, if they would get more than their allotted hour. As the discussion dwindled the group noticed that half an hour had gone. Excitement turned to agitation. Forty-five minutes elapsed. Agitation turned into anger. Hell! They had travelled around the world for enlightenment and she had stood them up.

With five minutes to go one of the group spoke of her disappointment. 'I've come all this way for what!' she spat out. At which the group heard a girlish chuckle from behind the tapestry screen. They turned and to their surprise saw Mother Teresa's face appear from behind it. She was grinning impishly.

'Thank God you have arrived,' someone said. 'Now we can speak with you. We have so many questions.'

Mother Teresa looked at her watch. 'My time is up.' She smiled. And with that she was about to leave the room.

'Wait!' someone said. 'You can't go, we have so much to ask you.'

'Well, I was here all the time.' Mother Teresa held out her hands helplessly. 'All you had to do was look for me.'

'But there is so much wisdom you can impart to us. Oh, please stay for a while longer.' The group pled in unison.

'Ah, wisdom is what you seek,' Mother Teresa echoed. 'Well, that will never leave you, it's been in the room with you all the time. Seek and you shall find.' With that she walked behind the screen and was gone.

The only difference between sick people and well people is that sick people have forgotten the memory that they are whole. What we focus on is what we create. The Nazarene focused on the divine creative essence of the cripple — and the cripple walked. Masters seem to be energy-efficient people. From the two examples so far neither master seems to have done anything.

Perhaps the third example, the Buddha, is different. Here was a man who became impassioned about finding enlightenment. So impassioned that he decided to sit under a Boa tree until he could find the switch that would turn on his enlightenment. The story goes that after a certain time the Buddha arose and declared that he had found it. He then proceeded to teach the path to enlightenment. I am unsure exactly how long he sat under this tree. Yet, I know that it was a shorter time than the time the Buddhist movement has been searching for the enlightenment switch.

Similarly, the Nazarene is purported to have healed the sick. He commanded his disciples to 'go out and do likewise'. This suggests that the healing process is simple. Yet the Christian movement, 2000 years on, is still having difficulty coming to grips with this simple statement.

Masters, throughout history, consistently show us that we are able just to do it ourselves. Whatever that *it* is. Yet their initiates struggle and toil to achieve the same objectives. We put processes into place in an attempt to ensure consistent outcomes. We place rules and regulations to protect the process that we believe to be divine. In doing so, we then distinguish between divine and human and suggest that we cannot be both at the same time. That is, we establish a paradoxical way of thinking. Then when we don't show our divinity we can say it was because we have broken the rules. We then can feel guilty that we have erred and go on a process of repentance to rid ourselves of the blocks to our divine expression. This is the realm of the MUST DO's. For hands-on healing to work I must put my hands in certain positions on the person's body. For faith healing to work I must believe. To become a Reiki healing master, an existing Reiki healing master must attune me.

Can you see how, as soon as we fall into the 'must do' world of conditions, we open ourselves to the possibility of other people, who claim to be more highly evolved, manipulating and controlling us? To place masters on pedestals suggests that we have forgotten the memory that we are whole and that we have forgotten the memory that we too are masters. To place masters above us and out of our reach then leads to a deification process that provides the meek with a reason to embark upon a mythical journey towards enlightenment. We then become trapped in a world of process, ritual and endless searching. This activity blocks our memories about our natures.

The notion that divinity and humanity are separate and therefore different is indeed the myth of the meek. Illness occurs when the soul has had enough of experiencing the personality's search along the mythical path to enlightenment. How do we know that the soul has had enough? Simply by experiencing the energy drain as the soul shuts off the power supply. As our batteries run down, illness manifests and we lose the desire to continue the mythical journey. This, I suggest, is an empowering moment when the personality can rest and choose to remember that the only difference between a sick person and a well person is that the sick person has forgotten the memory that they are whole. Therefore, when masters establish protocols of dependency on their particular processes to achieve wholeness then, in actuality, they are saying to people that they cannot see others' wholeness. To insist on the right and only process is demeaning. There is no soft way of saying this.

A few years ago my birthday — yes, masters actually age — was on a Saturday when I was running a 'Healing with Energies' workshop. On the Friday morning, as I was leaving home for the airport, Katrina slipped an envelope into my hand and whispered 'Happy Birthday'. I thanked her, then put the envelope into my pocket. Once on the aeroplane, I opened Katrina's envelope. Yes, it was a birthday card and on the front of the card it read: 'Do not follow where the path may lead. Go instead where there is no path and leave a trail'. Wisdom is always around us and taps us on the shoulder at the most unexpected times.

You see, the first part of the saying, 'Do not follow where the path may lead. Go instead where there is no path', is the affirmation of all masters. They know full well that the path to mastery is hidden from all but the one searching for their path. In this sense mastery is an aloneness path. It is certainly not lonely. Robert Johnson, a well-known Jungian analyst, says that the search for your Holy Grail can only be started at that part of the forest where no one has entered before. Masters' apprentices recognise that their journeys are unique and incomparable. You see, we can't show anyone else the way because the soul's roadmap is imprinted deep within its recesses.

The second part of the birthday card , '— and leave a trail,' suggests that people who leave trails are society's leaders. These people blaze the way so that other people can have an easier life. They have great intentions of doing good works. They always know that when you walk along another's pathway, the sights that you see are the experiences of others. In a sense, by walking on another's pathway, we become tourists. The ups and downs that we experience on the blazed trail (or the six-lane highways), although interesting, merely represent a ride through another's personality fun park. It might seem real at the time. I believe that our personal adventures begin when we leave the metaphysical Space Mountain of others' experiences and walk out the exit. Then we can decide to find the forest of our dreams and make our own path or queue up for the next Disney ride. Are you a master or a leader? If you are a master how then do you teach others? If you are a healer how do you heal others? Perhaps the masters know that to *sacrifice oneself in the service of satisfying others' needs is not serving them.*

Chapter 5

The Storyteller 3

'G'day, sir. Champagne, orange juice or water?' G'day. Ted had forgotten that people actually speak like that. He'd spent thirteen weeks in the United Kingdom listening to exclamations of 'bollocks', 'let's get this sorted', or other everyday speak. Ted chuckled as he remembered losing himself in the passion of a workshop at Southampton.

'We are all the creators of our reality,' he said. 'We are so good at it that all we have to do is focus on what we want to create for an instant and we get it. Well, perhaps not immediately because we need to allow time for the universe to put it together. Yet it will happen. That is the power of our intent. We are drawn to what we focus on. You have to understand this. We always create into the physical form whatever we focus on. Consider, for example, that the notion of original sin was created simply by focused intention. That's right, the biblical parable of Adam and Eve. Here are two people living in perfection. They are immortal, had all their needs cared for. One day while walking through the garden a snake pops out of a tree and says, "G'day".' The audience roared, laughing at Ted's unabashed reversion to his Australian heritage. It went over like a dream. As for Ted, he quietly remonstrated with himself for letting his guard down.

'I'll have the orange juice, thanks.' Ted reached for the glass on the steward's tray. 'Been in England long?' came the curt Australian accent.

'Not long enough!' Ted blurted out. 'I mean, I didn't see all that I wanted to.'

'You'll look forward to coming back then?' the steward continued. Ted had never satisfied himself that airline conversation was heartfelt. 'They get paid to do that,' he told his daughter once. Just like the serpent in the branches offering an illusion, so stood the steward with silver tray in hand, offering friendship.

'Now, everyone blames the serpent for bringing down perfection,' Ted continued. 'Yet reality is that Adam and Eve created their ignorance and imperfection simply by acknowledging it with their intent. Let's take a closer look at the scene. Rewind the video and put it into slow mo'. "Do you want to have more knowledge than you already have?" the snake asked. Now here is the trap. Adam and Eve are perfect. They are gods. They have everything, know everything. They are immortal! Yet, the snake has suggested that they might not be and Eve, by reaching out for the fruit, refocused her intention on the possibility that the snake might be right, that perhaps she was not perfect. Moreover, in that act she focused on the truck. In this case, the truck represented the possibility to her that she might be ignorant and somehow in a deficit state. In addition, to show how God-like she was, she created her imperfection, immediately. The story continues that humanity was banished from the garden and has been striving to find its perfection ever since. Why? Because humanity has forgotten that it is divine. Each time we reach for something offered to us that we believe we can't create in our own right, then we reinforce our belief that we can't have what we want. We create our own special brand of lack.'

Ted reached out for the glass on the silver platter. For a moment he silently lamented that he would be unable to afford business class for a very long time.

'Sir, your orange juice,' the steward said courteously, hiding his confusion.

Yes, Ted had reached for the glass. Yet, his hand fell limply from his arm, resembling a construction crane parked for the night.

'Sir, refreshment or not!' the steward pushed.

Ted looked up and thought he detected a reddish glint shining from the steward's eyes. The sunlight streamed through the opposite porthole making an effective stage back light, or was it the steward's aura? Ted looked into the haze and thought that he could see, ever so faintly, a pair of wings.

'Sir!' the steward's tongue flicked the word out with venomous intent.

'Shit! Where are the fangs?' Ted's mind raced in the background. He stared at the steward in disbelief as the red glint from the steward's eyes turned into headlights. The pilot revved the starboard engines just like the roar of a Pan Tech. The serpent had transformed into an oncoming truck. Ted shuddered, then spoke calmly to the steward. 'No thank you,' he said, withdrawing his arm. 'I'll save it for the next trip. I *will* be back next year.'

'Very well, sir.' The steward nodded, mumbling something under his breath and reinforcing Ted's view that courtesy is a paid commodity on aeroplanes.

Ted relaxed deep into the chair musing how easy it is to create trucks. Just listen to outside advice. He reflected on the many well-meaning snippets of advice that carried the serpent's venom. 'Any time and any place. Next year is going to be an excursion through snake country. Better stay focused.' Ted closed his eyes, feeling safe in the knowledge that no creditors could get to him for the next twenty hours. Economy passengers were still boarding so it would be a while before they took off. Nothing to do except dose.

'I have a dream,' Ted sometimes told his audiences. It was a good opener for a seminar. After all, it worked for Martin Luther King. Ted's was a different type of dream. Perhaps it would be better to replace the word 'dream' with the thought, 'I wish I had the courage to do it'. The dream went like this: he was an internationally acclaimed speaker and also successful. He was up there with the best and attracted crowds in the thousands. His dream topic was self-assertiveness. That's right! If you are self-assertive you can get anything you want at the time you want it. Just snap your fingers and hey presto! He would do one-day events where he would teach people the 'ancient secret self-assertiveness formula'.

Ticket prices would be set between $6000 and $20,000. Reasonable, and cheap really, when this day would change people's lives forever. Imagine getting what you wanted. Being who you wanted to be. Doing everything your heart desired. Being truly divine, a totally conscious creator of reality. Just imagine going from initiate searching to god in six hours! As the story unfolded, Ted sold the dream.

'Imagine the day. An auditorium packed to capacity. Six thousand people all aspiring to greatness. Feel the energy it would produce. Now, hear the motivational music seducing the audience into total involvement with the spiritual firework display.' The much smaller audiences he told the story to quickly envisaged the day that they would be in the audience secretly hoping to find their own self-assertiveness switch. 'Now picture the stage. All I want is a small table set in the middle of a stage. It has a solitary chair behind it. There, placed in the centre of the table, is an open book.

'The announcer introduces me to raise the energy to ethereal levels. "Ladies and gentlemen. Fellow masters of your destinies. I have immense pleasure in introducing you to Ted Ryan, master speaker and author of (titles peel off the announcer's tongue for the next five minutes). Please welcome to the stage the master of being himself: Mr Ted Ryan!"

'The stage blackens. The music changes to Vivaldi's 'Four Seasons' and a single spot lights up the table and the solitary book. A second spotlight falls on me and follows me as I walk across the stage and sit at the table. There I pick up a pen and begin to write my next book.' Ted pauses here for effect. Says nothing.

Usually, the silence is too much and an impatient person asks, 'What then?'.

Ted continues: 'I just do what I want to do — that's self-assertiveness. Sooner or later someone will get really annoyed. Chances are they will come out of the audience and demand their money back. At which point I give them the Self-assertiveness Mastery Certificate, tell the others that they have failed and get the hell out of there!'.

'Sorry.' A voice broke into his fantasy, the apology coming seconds after a sharp pain stabbed at Ted's foot.

Ted looked up. 'That's okay,' he replied to the elderly gentleman who was now settling into the seat next to him.

'I always go for the emergency exits,' the man said. 'More leg room.'

Ted looked into the face mouthing polite words of conversation. 'Well, he's not paid to be pleasant,' Ted thought. 'Then again, he is stuck next to me for quite a while. He probably wants to make the trip more bearable.' Ted noticed how the man's eyes shone when he spoke, though there was a tiredness behind them. 'Do you travel much?' Ted asked.

'Too much over the years.' The man puffed as he pulled his stomach in to secure the seatbelt. 'I am retired now but I still travel. I follow my children around the world as they move from job to job. Upwardly mobile they are. Have families. They don't stay in one place for more than a few years at a time. It was different in my day. Get a job and stick to it. Longevity and reliability were how we worked our way to the top. These days the tactic is job hop to success. Sell yourself to the highest bidder. They're great kids, all successful professionals. Yet at the same time they are business mercenaries. They never sit still.'

The man's face continued to draw Ted in. There were lines flaring majestically from the corners of his eyes. Ted thought that they looked like the sun's rays. Yet the corners of his mouth held past memories revealing deep glacial-like ravines hinting at unresolved sadness. His hair was neatly manicured. That's the right word. It was sculptured, crafted and styled. He was obviously wealthy and spoke well, yet without breeding. The man's hands suggested a toughness of character that showed he knew when to make hard decisions and act on them.

Ted's friend Rob, a successful property evaluator, had once told him: 'Buddy, in business you draw a line between yourself and everyone else. Then you promise yourself that if anyone puts a foot across the line you will cut it off! The decision you make is how close to you that you will draw the line'. Rob was very one-eyed about business. The gentleman sitting next to Ted hinted at the same qualities in his features.

'Good afternoon, ladies and gentlemen, and welcome to Qantas Flight 2 to Sydney via Bangkok. Shortly we will be pushing back from the terminal.'

The plane jolted like a helpless fish snagged on the end of a fishing line as it was towed away from the terminal. Keen cabin crew swarmed up and down the aisles like beagle hounds trained to sniff out drugs at luggage collection points. They collected cups and scrupulously looked into each passenger's private parts for a final seatbelt check.

'My name is Bob Rose.' The elderly gentleman propelled his large, gnarled hand towards Ted. Ted extended his and lost his mitt into the vice-like jaws.

'Ted Ryan,' he replied and looked full into Bob's face. In that moment Ted understood Bob. It was not intellectual. It was more like a feeling or a knowing. They say you can read a person by his face. Bob's surely was the road map to a life full of experiences. Yet, it was in the handshake that the feeling came. 'Handshakes,' Ted mused silently, 'are the communications link to the soul'.

He reflected back to the first real job he won after leaving the Australian Public Service. It was a headhunting position with a recruitment firm, 'Gateway People'. The owner, a rampant liberal, maintained emphatically that the firm served humanity by acting as the bridge between career moves. Ted warmed to the concept yet cooled to the job after a few initial wins.

The recruitment industry was moving quickly towards psychological testing as a scientific means to validate the headhunter's initial appraisal of candidates. Hiring had become a professional process extra-ordinaire. To the cynic, it seemed that the increase in scientific/behavioural appraisals could be linked to the rapid rise in headhunting fees. Ted found the process long, arduous and frustrating. The appraisals always — at least 90 per cent of the time — confirmed his original feeling while shaking the candidate's hand in greeting. For Ted, the appraisal took less than thirty seconds. The rest of the process included the first interview, the creation of the long list, reducing the long list to a short list. Writing appraisals and reference checking created a process that pretended to justify the fee. All that was required, he thought, was for the recruiter to say, 'This is the right person for the job'. He explained his philosophy to Warren, the owner of Gateway, who confidentially confessed that he also used his feelings.

'Ted, how you do it is of no concern to me, provided you are accurate,' Warren counselled. 'Our clients want some perceived value for their money, so we give them the process to justify our fees. It's that simple. We are considered the experts in our field. We are the masters of recruitment. That's why they pay big money.'

Ted had difficulty with the rationale. After all, the client could save more money than the fee by hiring a person quickly rather than having the process leave the position vacant for two months or more. It just didn't make sense. The object of the exercise was to hire staff. Yet the process prevented that from happening quickly. Ted was eventually fired. Warren caught him falsifying his recruitment briefs.

'I can handle most things,' Warren said as he was helping Ted pack his meagre belongings into a cardboard box. 'God, Ted! You have so much potential. Why have you thrown it down the toilet by lying?' Then as the lift doors were closing Ted heard Warren say to Pauline, his manager: 'Why does he have to tell stories? He could have been one of the best if he had only stayed with the process'.

QF 2 came to a stop mid-runway. 'I have an uneasy feeling about this,' Bob said as the captain began transmission.

'Ladies and gentlemen, we have discovered a problem in one of our starboard engines. We will return to the terminal where the ground engineers can run a safety check.'

Bob grunted, reached for his carry bag and went to change into a tracksuit. On his return, he nudged Ted. 'I had a quiet word with the head steward. The airline has changed since I ran it. The only problem they have is that the fail-safe computer system has failed.'

Ted looked confused. 'What does that mean?' he asked.

'Basically,' Bob went on, 'the process of checking whether the engine has failed or not has failed. There is nothing wrong with the engine at all. It's the system that tests the system that tests the engine that has failed. So they have delayed the flight because they can't tell if anything is wrong with the test system!'

'So how do you know that the engines are working properly?' Ted quizzed.

'Ah, that's easy, the engine warning lights are directly linked to the cockpit in case something like this happens.'

'So there's nothing wrong then?' Ted persisted.

'Only with the system process,' Bob replied. 'If they focus on the systems then that's all they will see. Forget the bloody results. Just promote the systems. More jobs that way.'

Chapter 6

Four Case Studies

Margaret

I met Margaret in one of those mysterious ways that some people call destiny. I had been reading a five-volume anthology called *Life and Teachings of the Masters of the Far East*. Baird T Spalding, the author, maintained that he represented a team of twelve scientists who studied the 'Masters' in the Far East for several years at the turn of the twentieth century. The books are controversial. They report miracle after miracle, manifestation and materialisation, time travel, and, of course, healings — with the odd resurrection thrown in.

The events reported in the pages struck a chord in my heart while my head kept yelling: 'Where is the proof? These things can't be true'. To which my heart quietly replied, 'What happens if they are possible?'. Every time I turned a page the debate was on. My Virgoan sun adopted the stance that nothing in the books was logical. My Aquarius ascendant took exception to Virgoan rationalism, asking 'What is logic anyway?' and my Sagittarius moon said, 'What the hell. Will you guys get it together so we can party?'. I could not put the books down, yet my inner turmoil grew to volcanic proportions. I had to solve the riddle, and the only way I knew how was to put it out to the universe and ask for proof. As a hands-on healer, several reports of healing particularly impressed me. So, taking a deep breath, I asked to meet and work with a person that modern medicine diagnosed as terminally ill. That's right. I wanted someone that the professionals had written off, someone I could practise on by using the techniques described in the books. Perhaps, if I was lucky, I could witness a healing miracle.

Time passed and I forgot about the request. Then one morning I answered a knock at the door from three strangers. A man introduced himself as a friend of a friend who attended my psychic development classes. He introduced his wife and then introduced Margaret, a close friend from Europe. They wondered if they could discuss Margaret's situation with me. Fortunately a client had just cancelled so I had time. As we sat on the lounge the man told me that Margaret had cancer. The doctors estimated that she had twelve weeks to live. Could I help?

They say we get what we ask for. I can assure you that at that moment I hoped for a metaphysical take-back law that I could use. 'Margaret doesn't understand anything about hands-on healing, so could you give her a demonstration?' the man asked.

'I guess so,' I weakly replied. That's how it started. I positioned Margaret on a chair in my lounge room. Her friends sat around her and I commenced a healing session.

When I work with my hands I like to use my fingertips as well as the palms. I prefer to start in the head region. It seems to relax the client quickly. I still remember how neatly Margaret's hair was styled. There was not a hair out of place. So, not wanting to disrupt her hairstyle (she had enough to worry about), I carefully placed my fingers through her hair so that they could rest on her scalp. The fingertips on my left hand found their marks and I proceeded to do the same with my right. Only this time my fingers kept on going and going. They didn't come to rest where the scalp was supposed to be. Rather they came to rest approximately two inches into her head!

Very embarrassed, I pulled my right hand away. Margaret sensed my discomfort and gently put up her hand, found mine and directed it back into the crevice.

'Don't worry Bruce,' she said. 'I had a tumour there several years ago and they had to take it out. That's why I have the situation in my lungs. It is a secondary growth.'

Indeed, she was right. Her hairstyle cleverly covered a previous operation. The best way I can describe it is that the surgeon took out a wedge, just like a wedge from an orange, out of her head. The drama over, I continued the healing session and an hour later Margaret reported having felt something and asked if I would visit her once a week to continue the healing. I agreed and, although my embarrassment over the discovery left me, something still bothered me. It bothered me so much that I knew I would have to ask her for an answer when the time felt right.

Each week I caught the ferry across Sydney Harbour to her serviced apartment in the city. I would deliver the energy she required and we talked about her life, philosophy and in a very short time became friends. By the third visit my curiosity was at its peak. So while I worked with her I asked the question that had nagged at me ever since we met.

'Margaret, there is something that I need to know, if you want to tell me,' I tentatively broached the subject.

'What's that?' she replied.

'Well, as you know, I am not a doctor and know very little about medical matters. Yet I have been wondering how you can still function fully with a part of your brain taken out.'

Margaret grinned impishly. 'The doctors told me that as well. In fact, they said that after the operation I would probably lose a lot of body function.'

I paused, hoping that she would continue, until I could wait no longer. 'What did you do when they told you? How did you feel?'

'Oh,' she said, 'I had a plan of my own. Just before they were to take me into surgery I explained to my brain that it was going to lose a part of its functionality. I respectfully told it that I had lots more to do with my life. Then I asked it to relocate all the vital functions and memories from the place where they were going to remove the growth to somewhere safe.'

It was silent in her lounge room. I could hear the ferries

pulling in and leaving Circular Quay.

'In fact,' she continued, 'as the anaesthetist was inserting the intravenous into my hand, I told the surgeon that everything would work out okay. I asked him not to worry because I had spoken to my brain.

'Can you imagine the scene? One of Europe's top surgical teams is about to embark on a life-threatening high-risk procedure and the patient tells them not to worry because she has fixed the problem!'

'How did they react?' I asked.

'They thought it was the pre-medication cutting in. The last words I heard from the surgeon were: "Well, I hope that you are right. Then again, if you are not, you won't know anyway".'

Let's pause here and reconsider the notion that what we focus on we create. Here, Margaret is faced with a huge truck coming down the highway. It's called cancer and behind that truck is another, equally as large. The second truck is the surgical procedure. Margaret, knowing that she was the driver of her car, realised that she had to ignore the blinding headlights of the oncoming trucks and focus on where she wanted to go. So, she steered her car, by telling it where she wanted to go. Obviously she passed the trucks because she was sitting in a chair in front of me fully functioning.

'When I came out of the anaesthetic,' she continued, 'I wiggled my toes. They seemed to work. Then I called out to the nurse and when she heard me I knew I had made it. Believe me, I thanked my brain most profusely.' She laughed.

'What about the surgeon?' I asked.

'Oh, he said that I was lucky and that no real miracle had happened. I just thought myself well.'

What a statement! How many times have you heard of miraculous healings and the medical professions criticise the event by unconsciously stating the truth. 'They only thought themselves well.' As for me, I realised why Margaret had come into my life. She was indeed the Master Healer, and I? I was the master's apprentice. After I left that day, I sat on the ferry humbled beyond words, yet thankful that I had asked the question of a terminally ill person.

William Blake, the great English poet, wrote: 'I must create a system or be enslaved in another man's. I must not reason nor compare. My business is to create'. Throughout this chapter, I will quote this passage frequently because it is the essential mission statement of the initiate seeking self-mastery. 'I must create a system or be enslaved by another person's.' Let's examine the ramifications of William Blake's words by following Margaret's story some more.

A few weeks later, my curiosity surfaced again. 'What is it like to be told by a doctor that you are going to die?' I asked Margaret.

She looked at me with a gleam in her eye that I now knew was a trademark of her defiance. 'When I was told I had lung cancer and had a short time to live, it was a very sad day,' she told me.

I agreed that it must have been a shock.

'Oh no!' she said sincerely. 'I wasn't sad. It was my doctor. He was crying. He was a friend and was very upset.'

'Well, what about you?' I asked.

'I just laughed.'

'Laughed?'

'Yes, laughed. It was sweet seeing him upset over something that just wasn't true.'

'How did he react when you laughed?' I asked.

'Well, he recommended that I consult a psychologist. He thought that I was in denial and needed to be convinced I was terminally ill.'

Here is a doctor saying that another truck is coming down the highway. Margaret agreed with him, yet when she says it won't kill her, science prevails and she is referred to a psychologist to convince her that she will hit the truck. William Blake again: 'I must create a system or be enslaved in another person's'. This statement relates to every facet of life — not just Margaret's more graphic example. The doctor is functioning within the guidelines of the medical system. He is saying that according to his system, Margaret will die within months. Indeed, according to the medical system this observation is correct. Yet Margaret has a decision to make. Either to accept another person's system and the resulting consequences or create her own. If she chooses to live in another person's system then, in effect, she is allowing someone else to drive her car. She has abrogated her responsibility and therefore becomes a victim to another's philosophical viewpoints.

'I must create a system or be enslaved in another person's.' William Blake knew full well that the wages of sin is death. What is the definition of sin? I suggest that it is asking, or allowing, someone else to drive your car. What is the definition of death? Perhaps it is the loss of our drive to create. If we allow another to drive our car repeatedly then over time we forget how to drive. We lose the skill. When we cease creating in our lives we lose the skill and forget that we can create. Once we have forgotten that we can create we also forget who we are. We forget the memory that we are whole. Our personality then becomes disassociated from our creative essence or our soul. We move from Adam and Eve in the Garden of Eden where they had every need met, to Adam and Eve working for a living and hoping that they had enough superannuation to cover their retirement until they died.

'I must create a system or be enslaved by another man's. I must not reason nor compare. MY BUSINESS IS TO CREATE.' In Margaret's situation the reasoning process was based on medical tests and trials. Yet they were reasoned systems that related to other people's systems not to hers. In her own special way, Margaret created her health because she focused on the road past the truck or the desire to continue creating in this life.

'That's why I came out to Australia,' she continued. 'I just couldn't face the session with the psychologist.'

I began to believe that Margaret would heal herself. I also came to understand my role. As a healer I actually cannot heal any one other than myself. In that sense we are all healers. It was Margaret's responsibility to heal herself. My role was as an external device to allow her to state her intention into the physical realm where the health problem existed. Even her doctors and surgeons acted in this manner. Each time she told them what her system was, they provided the opportunity for her to express her creative intention.

Somewhere in our association I had given her Louise Hay's famous book, *You Can Heal Your Life*. Louise's personal story is an inspiration to all who read it. Her book is typically a 'how-to' book with valid steps to return to health and wellbeing. She also has a chapter on her personal healing process. At one of Margaret's sessions I was sitting on the floor giving healing to Margaret's feet. An apt position in retrospect.

'Have you read the book I gave you?' I quizzed.

'Oh yes, it's wonderful!' Margaret exclaimed. 'I've included it in my library of special books.' She pointed to a shelf where five books were stacked. I could see Louise's book on the top of the shelf. It had radically changed appearance. The book had reduced its thickness by about 90 per cent. Curious, I walked over to the book, picked it up and opened it. Margaret had ripped out all the chapters except the chapter relating Louise's personal healing story.

'That's right.' Margaret read my mind. 'I realised that the inspirational quality of the book was about a woman who overcame cancer her way. I then realised that if I tried to heal myself Louise's way then I would be untrue to myself. I have to heal myself my way.' That is why she kept the chapter in the book, as inspiration when she needed hope. I realised yet again that I was sitting at the feet of a master. What became of Margaret? She returned to Europe and, at the time of writing, is still going strong. It has been about five years since we last met. Yet I still hear from her sporadically or via her referring friends. Did I heal her with my magic healing hands? I think not. My contribution as a healer was to provide support to a person wanting to create a personal system.

What a success story! In those days it was my desire to create successful healings. I used to joke that we healers should stamp each success on the doors of our practice rooms the same way fighter pilots stamped kills on their planes. When I spoke about healings, business associates would suggest that I document and publicise them. 'Great for business,' they usually exclaimed. However, publicising them generated two problems for me. Firstly, people might ask for sessions with expectations that I could heal them. Sounds silly, I know, yet true. A major problem that healers face is that their clients expect they can heal them! Put this scenario into our driving analogy. The client has booked in for a driving lesson with the expectation that the driving instructor will drive the car for them. If this happens then clients become enveloped in the healer's system and do not develop theirs. As a healer, I must not teach a client to drive my way. Rather, my role is to encourage them to drive cars their way.

The second problem arising from publicised success stories is that often our definition of success is just a statement about the conclusions of our system and has no bearing on another's system. If I define a healing success as a physical cure, then I establish a system that carries with it laws that are conditional. That is, a successful healing is one that results in a person regaining physical health. I believe that we incarnate into the physical realm to face our gravest fear that we are not whole and to discover the reality that we are.

CASE STUDY 2   # Joyce

The definition of wellness contains many assumptions. How do we know when a person is healed? How do we know when we are successful healers? What is the definition of illness? As we proceed through *Healing Energies*, the answers to these questions are, I believe, the hidden diamonds in the desert, treasures that dedicated healing masters (that's everyone) occasionally stumble across. A diamond has many facets and as we continue on our journeys we experience different facets of healing. Therefore, what may be obvious to you may be hidden from someone else. I believe that it is via our life's experiences that we go diamond mining. Life's experience is the spotlight and the evaluation equipment.

The next case study exemplifies this point.

ACT ONE, SCENE ONE: Joyce, the leading lady, appears on stage. She is successful and affluent, nearing sixty years of age, with a grown family and every reason to look forward to living out her retirement happily and prosperously. Until, at a routine medical examination, she discovers she has terminal cancer. The doctors commence chemotherapy. She becomes involved in a cancer support group and somehow finds her way into my healing rooms.

ACT ONE, SCENE TWO: The healings become a regular weekly event and within a month to six weeks the results from her tests suggest that she is going into remission. That's right! It looks as though I can stamp another victory on the door. The cancerous growth is shrinking and the doctors become ever so slightly optimistic, thus reinforcing the drive for more healing sessions. Several months later medical tests show no signs of the cancer. Joyce is cured! Let's pick up the play at Act One, Final Scene before the interval break. Joyce and I have just finished a healing session. As she comes out of a meditative state:

BRUCE: It is wonderful news, Joyce. Ridding the cancer. It's quite a victory. Must be such a weight off your mind.

JOYCE: I suppose so. (*Joyce is uninterested, looks down at the floor.*)

BRUCE: You don't seem very pleased. This is great news. Your family must be relieved.

JOYCE: (*Unenthusiastically*) Oh. I guess they are. My husband slept the whole night for the first time since I was diagnosed. The children can now get on with their lives. Yet, for me. Well, I just don't know.

BRUCE: Don't know?

JOYCE: Yes. Strange really. I wanted so much to get well. I was really scared of dying. I remember how terrified I was when the doctor told me. Death, it was such a cold, clammy depressive concept to face.

BRUCE: Well, there is no need to worry about that now.

JOYCE: That's the point. Somewhere during the healing sessions I realised that there is nothing to fear from dying. That dying is just the transition process from one state to another. I realised that I am perfectly safe no matter what state I am in.

BRUCE: I … I don't understand.

JOYCE: Bruce, it no longer matters to me if I live or die. If the cancer came back tomorrow it wouldn't phase me like it did before. All I want to do before I die is

see my daughter happily married. She is engaged to
a wonderful boy. They are planning to marry in
about six months.

The curtain drops for intermission. Act Two begins with Bruce
believing that he is a failure and that Joyce has lost her will to live.
Joyce stops coming for healing because it just doesn't matter
anymore. The time passes and we move into the final scene. Bruce
is at a railway station waiting for a train and meets Jerry, the
person who referred Joyce to him.

BRUCE: Jerry, I haven't seen you in ages. What brings you
            back to Sydney?

JERRY: Didn't you know? Joyce died last week. The
            memorial service was this morning.

BRUCE: Sorry to hear that. What a pity. She was doing so well.

JERRY: Yes, that's what we all thought. Quite tragic really.
            She was in total remission with no sign of cancer at
            all. Even two days before her daughter's wedding, she
            received the medical all clear. I can tell you that
            really made the wedding special.

BRUCE: What happened? How did it return?

JERRY: Quick! It was so fast. The day after the wedding her
            daughter and new son-in-law came over on their
            way to London. They had work over there. Anyway
            Joyce and the family took them to the airport. It was
            a happy farewell. It was all so quick and unexpected.

BRUCE: Go on.

JERRY: Well, the morning after the kids flew out, Joyce woke up with a pain in her side. She went to the hospital. The cancer had reappeared and she died that evening.

BRUCE: Was she in much pain?

JERRY: Her husband said that at the time she passed on he could not remember when she looked more peaceful. He said that there was a special radiance about her. He said that it was the sort of look that comes just after a person has succeeded at something after a hard struggle.

The curtain closes for the final time and the audience is left to ponder the questions.

Does healing really work? What did Joyce really need healing from? Was it the belief that death was frightening and horrid? Human tragedies are full of inspirational ironies. In order for Joyce to conquer her fear of death, she first had to face the possibility that she might hit the truck. The story-line leads the audience to believe that the truck, in this instance, symbolises death. Yet the truck, in reality, was Joyce's fear of dying.

So that Joyce could continue travelling on her side of the road, she had to focus on the road past the truck and to her destination. Joyce, the creator of the play and lead actor, wrote the play so that she could only reach the destination by travelling through the gates of physical death. The gates straddled a two-lane highway with each lane carrying trucks travelling in opposite directions. Each lane represented choices. The highway also carried a truck travelling at speed towards Joyce from the opposite direction. The sign at the front of the truck was lit up, since it was carrying a dangerous payload. The sign said, 'DANGER'. This truck is carrying False Expectations Appearing Real. The truck's identification plates were personalised. They carried the word 'illusion'. Joyce chose to travel at night so that the glare from the truck's headlights hid its identification.

William Blake again: 'I must create a system or be enslaved in another person's. I must not reason nor compare. My business is to create'. In Joyce's situation, she, as with all of us, wrote her life's story. She defined the plot. She developed the rules of the game. She acted in the one and only performance. As with most writers, the plot or the main thread of the story faded from consciousness as she developed the play. To complete the play and receive a standing ovation she needed to remember what she originally wanted to create. Therefore, she consulted a healer. A person who knew how to bring lost memories back into consciousness. Note that the healer had developed a system for regaining memories. It was not a system to tell Joyce how to write the play. The healer knew that to recover the lost memory, the playwright needed to be encapsulated in love, for a time, protected from outside distraction, so that she could allow the memory of the story concept to resurface in its chosen time.

If my system defined successful healing as physical cure then clearly my system failed. If my system wrote story-lines and I told Joyce what her story-line should be then I had manipulated Joyce's thought processes and had taken on the responsibility of writing Joyce's play. Joyce's creative self would become suppressed until the memory of its creative purpose was lost. Joyce, the creator, had not died. All that was lost was the memory that she was the playwright. If she tried to live according to other people's systems (unless that was her chosen story-line) then her life would become an illusion and disassociated from her creative essence (soul). I suggest that creating is a human obsession. Therefore, the creator in us will not lie down and die. It will reach a point where it suggests to its physical colleague to slow down so that it can recap on the play that it wants to create. I believe that we witness this suggestion process as the manifestation of what we popularly call disease. Disease then truly takes on the interpretation given to it by so many today of dis-ease of our creative essence.

Andrew

The next case study is one that always brings a tear to the eye when I tell it in the workshops. It begins when a friend approached Katrina and asked her to visit Andrew, approximately two years of age. Andrew had leukaemia. There are several stories here, so it will take some time to set the scene.

Healing Energies is a book that uses the healing systems of Reiki and Seichim as a way to illustrate the journey towards wellbeing. In the hands-on healing fraternities there are, as with most professions, intense jealousies. Usually these jealousies concern technique. Reiki schools will tell you that their system works best. They will also tell you that their energy is the purest healing energy. Seichim masters, for example, teach that the very word Seichim (Sekhem) translates into English as the 'power of powers'. Reiki masters also maintain that Reiki energy is the most powerful. As I attune people into both systems, I often think about how, if I believed the claims, I am attuning people into controversy and competing energies. Some spiritual healing schools consider that the Reiki fraternities are really nice people yet misguided in making such a claim. In fact, any group that has to put a label onto this process indicates that they want some type of distinction and exclusivity. William Blake's statement reflects a certain cynicism to such claims: 'I must create a system that works better than the rest. I must reason and compare otherwise how can I distinguish my importance. My business is to increase subscriptions to the best system on earth — mine'. Yes! I am cynical at times. It is not my fault, though. I am a Virgo. Systems of thought can be quite debilitating really.

My belief is, and of course I am right, that we create the energy that we require to heal when we need it. I don't subscribe to the channel philosophy that tells us that we are merely garden hoses, or channels, for this divine energy to travel along in order to reach the sick person. Rather, I believe that when we lay our hands on clients, they feel the eternal soul message that is quoted so often. It was the primary theme or story-line of the Nazarene, a true master. 'Be still and KNOW that I AM God'. When I know that I AM God then I remember that I AM whole and I heal. Anyway, that's my story and I am sticking to it.

When Katrina and I met she had little experience with psychics, spiritual healers, Reiki practitioners or hands-on healers. Ironically, I claimed all of these titles. Titles are great for filling in space on business cards. Shortly after we began living together a client gave her a book that changed her life, *Hands of Light* written by Barbara Brennan. It is a comprehensive and honest work on the subject. Katrina accepted the book and I noticed that during the days that followed she would disappear into a quiet part of the house and become absorbed in Barbara's book. *Hands of Light* became frayed, written in, annotated and digested in a most thorough manner. This is the way Katrina approaches her healing studies.

I watched this process from a distance until Katrina approached me and simply stated in her obtuse Aries manner, 'Bruce, I want to give this healing stuff a go'. I thought that her desire was great but it takes years of practice to perfect the art of healing. You just can't pick it up in a few weeks. Nevertheless, Katrina wanted to *take up her bed and walk* so I magnanimously offered her an observing role in my sessions. I was sure that I could teach her in a most appropriate and professional manner. During her first session, I asked her if she wanted to participate. 'Just take it slowly and put your hands here,' I suggested. Katrina began. The energy in the room shot up like a thermometer in a heat wave and I realised that I was actually redundant!

Katrina is now a Reiki and a Seichim master. I needed someone to practise on. I can still see the look of disappointment in her eyes after the attunements.

'Is something supposed to happen?' she asked. 'I didn't feel any difference.'

There you go. Bruce, the healing master, transformed into a deflated balloon and yet another reality struck home. Katrina didn't feel the difference because she already knew what it was like to be a healer. She didn't need someone to make her one. She simply created her healing energies through an intention stated some time before: 'Bruce, I want to try this stuff'.

I report Andrew's story here as an observer because he was Katrina's client. Andrew's stage play touched all of us in the audience. At the time Katrina met Andrew, he was undergoing chemotherapy. Her role was to give hands-on healing to him on a regular basis. Initially, this took place after each chemotherapy session. Because of Andrew's age, Angela, his mother, would call Katrina when Andrew was taking his daily nap. Katrina then went to his house and gave him the healing while he slept. The session usually took an hour. As time passed, Angela reported that often after Katrina's visits Andrew's energy levels increased and sometimes, although we cannot scientifically confirm this, it appeared that his blood cell counts improved.

Katrina occasionally commented that she felt that the hands-on healing was keeping Andrew alive while the chemotherapy tried to rid him of the cancerous cells. I mention this because there is a huge gulf between the medical professions and hands-on healers. Often it is a 'one-or-the-other' choice of whether to undergo medical treatment or to take advantage of hands-on healing energies. Here was an instance where there was a cooperative synergy established between the two approaches.

Andrew turned three. Everyone silently prayed that he was improving, and the therapies and treatment continued. Andrew would initially respond to the chemotherapy and to the hands-on healing, yet in the gaps during treatment he would relapse. He became a well-known personality at the hospital and formed many friendships there. Over the years that followed, I remember Katrina saying repeatedly that she believed that her role and that of the medical profession, was to keep Andrew alive until he decided what he wanted to do. You will notice the difference in Andrew's situation and the first two case studies. Here is a little boy who has not been barraged by life's belief systems. He has not left his creative path, yet he is immobilised and undergoing a medical process just like his adult counterparts.

Let's fastforward the video to Andrew's fifth birthday. He is now waiting for a bone marrow transplant, yet every time the doctors test him, they detect a rogue leukaemia cell that stalls the procedure. Christmas arrives and for the first time in two years Andrew has the opportunity to spend time with his family at home. His family is excited at the prospect, as indeed is Andrew. After Christmas lunch Andrew asks if he can go back to the hospital because his friends are having a party there. Over three years of his life Andrew had come to view hospital life as normal. His role models were people with balding heads due to chemotherapy, people who, when in hospital, live with tubes connecting them to drug dispensers.

What is Andrew's oncoming truck? What is written on the truck's identification plates? What does the road past the truck look like? Indeed, what is the creative pot of gold that the road is leading to?

While you are thinking about the answers, I want to tell you about a healing phenomenon that happens across all styles of hands-on healing. As the practitioner delivers the energy it is quite common that they drift into an ambient, peaceful state. In this state there is often a feeling that the energies of both practitioner and client blend in a most beautiful way. When this happens there seems to be a communication channel established between both parties where thoughts are exchanged. This communicative process is not verbal. I believe that this communication is at a soul-to-soul level. Occasionally during this process the following words seem to come through the practitioner: 'You can heal yourself now'; 'You can release this condition now'; 'It is safe to be whole'. The words may change, yet the essential meaning never does. It is during these sessions that occasionally the words, 'Take up your bed and walk' are said to the client. Sometimes a feeling similar to a clicking in of a dislocation happens. When it does I always know that the person has taken up their bed and is walking. Sometimes there is no response and I know that the memories of wholeness are still buried deep in the subconscious.

It was a sunny afternoon when Katrina came home after a session with Andrew. This time she was not smiling. There was an aura of sadness around her. I asked her how the session went.

'My job is finished with Andrew,' she replied.

'Why?' I asked.

'Because he doesn't want the healing any more. He has made the decision to die.'

'How do you know that?' I persisted.

'Well, he was asleep as usual when I treated him. Shortly into the session I felt the words come through me to him: "It's time to let the White Knights win".'

Now this is significant because the way that doctors at the hospital explain leukaemia to children is by using the analogy of a battle between white and black knights in shining armour, the black knights being the leukaemia cells and white knights being the healthy ones.

'Surely that's positive,' I said. 'The white knights are the good guys.'

'Yes, that's right, they are.' Katrina's mood remained the same. 'The problem is that when these words came through Andrew rolled away from me although he was still asleep.'

'How can you be sure it was a reaction to the words?' I reached for a straw of hope.

'Because the words came through at least five times and each time when they did, he rolled away. Bruce, I tell you my time is finished there.'

ACT TWO, FINAL SCENE: Andrew is at home snuggled in bed resisting the call to go to school. Angela enters to ask whether he wants breakfast.

ANDREW: Mummy, it really hurts. I just don't want to hurt any more.

ANGELA: (*She senses that this is different and calls Peter, her husband.*)

PETER: Andrew, are you okay?

ANDREW: Daddy, I don't want to hurt any more.

PETER: Well, Andrew, if you are staying alive because you don't want to upset your mum, brother and me, then I am saying that even if you go we will always love you.

Wow! Can you imagine the courage it took for Peter to say that and for Angela to support him? Where do people find wisdom like that? Sensing that Andrew was going to die, the family sat with him for an hour or so, after which time Andrew hugged everyone and quietly passed his truck.

When I reach this part in my workshops, I pause, partly to control the lump in my throat and partly to create the atmosphere for the next question. No, the lump in the throat part is not for Andrew. In telling this story I am always left in awe at the wisdom of his parents and the courage they displayed. The questions that I ask are these: Did the healing work? What was Andrew's truck? What trucks did his family have to face to continue on their journeys?

I agree that we can rationalise anything to find solace, especially when children seem to suffer unfairly. No-one takes joy in witnessing a young child suffering or leaving this dimension so quickly. Yet, although infant and child death seems tragic, I believe that these little people are indeed masters who, for reasons only known to them, choose a path of suffering to create the trucks for those they love. Somehow in the stories I hear of child death and disease, the people who are most serene are the children. They display so much wisdom and, in their childlike manners, display incredible trust in a process that seems so hidden from adults. During their suffering, we adults must reach inside ourselves to face our fears of the unknown. We must look into the darkness, past the oncoming truck, and move into it in order to move on. These children, through their suffering, create the trucks of experience and growth in our lives. And as a result of the love bonds between the people touched by such tragedy these trucks race towards us. Yet unlike the trucks of our making, these analogous machines will not stop until we are ready to pass by them. Rather they race headlong towards us forcing us to seek the endless opportunities held in the darkness created by the blinding light of their headlights. These trucks shout out the message to the families remaining to take up their beds and walk.

CASE STUDY 4   # Anthony

I have tabled three case studies thus far. One traditionally successful case study and two studies needing some rationalisation to claim healing success. The final case study is about Anthony, a successful businessman about fifty years of age. Anthony felt a slight discomfort in his side and mentioned it to his doctor at a routine examination. The doctor poked and prodded, hummed and ah'd then sent Anthony for more tests. Let's pick up the story in Act One, Scene Five. The setting is in the doctor's consulting rooms. Anthony and the doctor speak softly about current affairs. It is eleven o'clock in the morning on a day that heralds great hope as summer approaches. The doctor reaches into a file and pulls out a large manila envelope containing X-rays.

ANTHONY: What are those, Robert?

ROBERT: They are the X-rays from your tests. How have you been feeling lately?

ANTHONY: Okay, really.

ROBERT: And the pain in your side?

ANTHONY: (*Thinks for a moment.*) It's still there. It's not very sore. More like a dull bruising pain that just won't go away. Should I be worried about it?

ROBERT: No. Yet we do need to talk about it. Coffee? (*Robert buzzes the receptionist and orders two coffees.*) The situation that we have, Anthony, is that you have a growth here. (*Points to place on X-ray.*).

ANTHONY: (*Leans forward to get a closer look.*) What is it?

ROBERT: It's a tumour, Anthony. Cancer actually. The tests
             show it as malignant. (*The coffee arrives. The two
             look at each other in silence for a moment that spells
             out eternity.*) It's nothing to worry about.

ANTHONY: (*Leans back into chair and sighs in relief.*) That's
             good.

ROBERT: Yet we must talk it through. You have quite a
             challenge here.

The doctor then proceeds to explain to Anthony that the
growth is very close to the liver. He explains that if the cancer
continues growing at the observed rate then it will reach the liver
quickly.

ANTHONY: Well, what treatment do you suggest?

ROBERT: Anthony, there is no medical treatment. The
             situation is simply this. If the cancer reaches the
             liver you have about two weeks before the liver will
             stop functioning. When that happens you will not
             live for long.

ANTHONY: (*Laughs nervously, now in shock.*) But you told me
             that there was nothing to worry about. How long
             have I got?

ROBERT: As long as you want. Look, Anthony, what I am
             telling you is that according to all the medical
             studies and information about your condition, you
             have about a month of life left.

ANTHONY: Nothing to worry about!

ROBERT: That's right. All I am telling you is that my system of
           healing can't help you any more. So it's now up to
           you to heal yourself. I know you can do it because I
           have seen others heal. I am still here for you to carry
           out whatever tests that you deem necessary and as a
           friend. Yet you must know that I cannot heal this
           condition for you.

           END ACT ONE.

I was so touched by Anthony's plight when I heard about it
that I invited him, via mutual friends, to a 'Healing with Energies'
workshop as my guest. It was fortunate, I thought, because the
next workshop was in his vicinity. As I was preparing for it, the
telephone rang.

'Am I speaking to Bruce Way?' the voice inquired.

I said, 'Yes'.

'This is Anthony here. You generously invited me to your
workshop.' I was glad that he had rung, and told him that I was
looking forward to meeting him. 'Oh, I can't come,' he exclaimed.
'The reason that I am phoning is to thank you and to tell you that
I just don't have time to come. I have lots to do. Perhaps when
things settle down I will come to a future workshop.'

I remember thinking cynically that he was right. He didn't have
much time and lapsed into my judgmental Virgoan self. I decided
that Anthony was in denial and just not ready to take up his bed and
walk. I remember feeling disappointed. I think, in retrospect, that I
was hoping for a miracle cure that I could be associated with.

'That's a pity,' I replied. 'The workshop could help.'

Anthony laughed then said: 'Bruce, I am sure that it will. Yet I
really don't have the time. You see, when I found out about my
condition I realised that the one thing above all others that I
resented was that I hadn't spent enough time with my children. In
the time I have left all I want to do is to restore the balance. That's

it. Then, if I still have time, perhaps I can consider doing something like your workshop. People have been so wonderful to me, Bruce. I have so many offers of alternate therapies I just hope that I have time to try some'.

As I listened to Anthony I felt a strange peace come over me. 'Anthony, I have a feeling that you will never need healing from anyone else,' I heard myself say down the line. What a terrible thing to say! I thought. Yet it was true. Something in Anthony's attitude told me that he had already taken up his bed and was walking. 'If you like I will send you a copy of my book, *Living Intuitively*,' I offered, feeling ever so slightly insipid and useless.

'Thanks, Bruce, I would really appreciate that.'

I asked for his address.

'Look, sorry mate, I've gotta run. I am going to the movies with my daughter.' Click. The phone connection withered and died. Yet deep in my heart I knew Anthony had what it took and that any outside therapy might retard his healing process.

A month later, I heard from Anthony's friends that he had been given a reprieve from the doctors. They had conducted a fresh battery of tests and had revised their diagnoses from two weeks to two years of life left.

'It's amazing!' they declared. 'That in this day and age a doctor could misdiagnose like that.'

I smiled inwardly, knowing that Anthony had lifted up his bed. Three months later, I had the privilege to meet Anthony. 'How are you?' I asked as we shook hands.

'I'm fine, thanks.' Then he continued as if he had an afterthought. 'And so is the cancer.'

Now Anthony's last comment hit its mark and my face must have shown it.

'You are surprised at my remarks,' he laughed.

I nodded.

'I have been in enough conflicts to know that if I hate the enemy and try to destroy it then I will suffer collateral damage.

Frankly, Bruce, the damage is not worth it.' Anthony went on to explain that the cancer was indeed alive and well. 'The best way I know to handle this situation is for me to find a way that I can co-exist peacefully with the cancer.'

Once again I had found another master to teach me. When Anthony told me what his doctor had initially told him, I realised that there were two masters in the scenario and regretfully I was not one of them. Let's go back to the statement by William Blake. 'I must create a system or be enslaved in another person's. I must not reason or compare. My business is to create.' Do you remember the words of the doctor? Let's apply them to William Blake's statement.

ROBERT: That's right. All I am telling you is that my system of
            healing can't help you anymore. So it's now up to
            you to heal yourself. I know you can do it because I
            have seen others heal. I am still here for you to carry
            out whatever tests that you deem necessary and as a
            friend. Yet you must know that I cannot heal this
            condition for you.

Robert, in telling Anthony that he could no longer help him, actually pushed Anthony out of the medical system. To some that may seem cruel. Yet in this instance it empowered Anthony. Why? Because Robert also challenged Anthony with the Nazarene's saying in his own words. 'So it's now up to you TO HEAL YOURSELF.' There is certainly a *take up your bed and walk* flavour about Robert's challenge. Blake: 'I must create a system or be enslaved in another person's'. In Anthony's case there was a real possibility that he could become entrapped in a system where he believed he would die. Blake: 'I must not reason nor compare'. Tests tell Anthony that he is going to die in two weeks. How often do practitioners try to entrap us into their systems? Blake: 'I must not reason nor compare'. Why? Because it's 'my business to create'.

When I asked Anthony what it was like to be given the death sentence, he replied that it was the most inspiring moment that he could remember in his life. I met Anthony almost three years ago. The last time I spoke with him — about six months before writing this book — fresh medical tests showed that ... well, actually, they showed absolutely nothing. There was no growth, no cancer cells, no illness. I asked Anthony if he had any plans for the future.

He simply replied, 'Absolutely! I just want to maintain the balance'. And that's the way I want to finish this chapter. Let's keep Anthony's ambition in mind and ask two questions: Is illness merely a state of imbalance? If it is, then what creates the imbalance?

Chapter 7
The Storyteller 4

Ted thought it ironic that QF 001, his initiating flight, left Sydney for Heathrow three hours late. QF 001 was the beginning of the speaking tour that he thought would be so successful. In his mind, it had to be successful to give him the life he wanted, dreamt about and visualised obsessively. At the time, he thought that the delay was simply a manifestation of his unconscious resistance to abundant success. He thought that the delay was the universe's way of giving him a message to heal his attitude.

'Illness is like that,' he thought. 'It makes you slow down and do nothing. Yet the mind never stops. Perhaps the body slows so the mind can focus on the imbalance. Then that's a description of physical illness. What about behavioural?' He always avoided using the word 'mental'. 'What about financial? What about relationship dysfunction?' The questions never stopped in Ted's mind. He was part philosopher. He knew that. Yet whenever he thought that he had found the formula explaining a topic, the exception always rose from the murky depths of 'what ifs' to dispute his hypothesis. 'Do exceptions prove the rules?' he thought. 'Or do they...?'

Now Ted sat on QF 002. The flight that would return him to the problems that he thought he never had to face again. Yet instead of jetting him quickly to face the music the mechanical bird stood reluctantly still on a side runway. The problem preventing take-off was apparently buried deep within the aeroplane's electronic complexity. Every so often the captain tried to reassure the passengers but he had nothing to say, because no-one knew what the problem was. 'What is the universe telling me now?' Ted reflected. He tried to meditate, hoping that his spirit guides could explain the insanity of the past thirteen weeks. Why? Why? Why? It seemed to him that the spirit guide switchboard was also closed for repair or perhaps they were out to lunch.

'Ladies and gentlemen,' the captain's voice droned yet again over the intercom. 'We have patched the computer problem for now. So we will be resuming our position in the runway queue. I am waiting for a departure time from the tower. I trust it will be soon.'

Ted glanced at his watch. Three hours had gone. The same delay as before. 'What does this mean?'

Bob leant across and whispered in Ted's ear, 'What the captain is really saying is that they can't find the problem but even if they did it wouldn't affect our safety.'

'God, not now,' Ted thought. 'I'm just on the verge of understanding and this guy …' Ted grunted to get Bob off his back. He felt guilty about it yet it had to be done. Ted also felt that Bob knew that he had fobbed him off. He suspected that Bob was able to see the subtle truths in life often hidden in a deluge of rhetoric or body language.

'What brought you to England?' Bob tried to start a conversation.

'Business.' Ted parried the question. No point in going over old ground, he thought.

'Do any sightseeing in between meetings?' Bob tried another approach. Ted was a challenge and Bob loved a good chess game.

'Yes, I saw a bit,' came the curt response.

'What appealed to you the most?' Bob moved a verbal pawn to within attack range of Ted's outer defences.

'I loved Edinburgh. Amazing really. From the moment I stepped into the cab at the airport I felt that I was home. I have never had an experience like it.'

Bob smiled, knowing that his pawn had reached Ted's outer perimeter. Ted, on the other hand, realised that he had said too much and plucked the in-flight magazine from the seat pocket.

'You won't find that as interesting as Edinburgh.' Bob slipped his bishop through Ted's pawn defences. 'Experiencing first-hand is the go.' Bob pushed the advantage.

'Oh, I don't know. It can be safer at arm's length,' Ted replied, remembering advice from another time. The game now in full swing. Ted realised that Bob was not going to concede so he reluctantly entered the game.

'Safer, yes. But what's the point of safe?' Bob continued. 'If you haven't tried, you haven't died and if you haven't died then you have no idea how to live.' If Bob was a fisherman he had baited the hook perfectly. Introduce even a hint of a philosophical discussion and Ted could not resist. He leant into the conversation. Bob sensed the engagement and continued. 'I can't count how many times I have failed. Or rather thought I failed in my life. Often, after the serious failures, I vowed that I would pull my horns in and just exist. Stop taking risks and be content with what I had. The problem was that, once the pain of the failure subsided and the wounds healed, I just had to try again. How could I ever know if my ideas would work if I didn't have a go?'

'But what if you believed so much that your ideas were right and then everything conspired to bring you down?' Ted asked.

Bob rubbed his forehead and frowned. 'Sounds like you have had a recent dose of failure. Now that I am through my life I look back at all the mistakes I made and I know.' Bob began to browse the in-flight menu. Had Ted known better, he would have thought that Bob was selling him by using the oldest sales ploy in history — the pregnant pause. Throw out the fishing line. Get the person interested and then pause creating a silence full of hope.

'Know what?' Ted wanted to deliver the baby.

Bob looked up from the menu. 'I wish Qantas would get off this nouveau food kick. It might taste good but God! It is difficult to keep on a fork.'

The two men just stared at each other, Bob now totally distracted and Ted wanting answers. 'Bob, you were saying?' Ted moved his knight into the fray.

Bob looked disoriented then quickly focused. 'Ah, yes. That all my mistakes were simply misinterpretations of the Thread Theory.' Bob smiled and pencilled his choices for dinner.

'What is the Thread Theory?' Ted asked.

'You won't find it in management books.' Bob shuffled in his seat. 'And I can't explain it to you either. It's something that you have to discover yourself.'

'Can you give me a clue at least?' Ted asked.

'It's all to do with success, healing and knowing who you are,' Bob went on. 'Illness is only a dysfunctional state that affects more than physical health. It affects every facet of life. The person who can't manage finances and the person who unwillingly hops from relationship to relationship are examples. In fact, any facet of life that a person is unhappy about could be called illness.'

'We seem to have made a huge jump here.' A sharper, critical tone crept into Ted's voice. 'From business success to healing. I don't understand the connection.'

Bob smiled. 'That's where the Thread Theory comes in. Find the thread and you find the connection.'

'Yet you say you cannot explain the Thread Theory to me.' Ted's patience had ebbed.

'You find the Thread Theory in the telling of your life's story. The only way that I can help you is to listen to your story. If you want to share it with me.'

'I wouldn't know where to start,' Ted replied.

'Start from today and work backward. What brought you to the UK on business?' Checkmate! Bob had Ted where he wanted him.

'I have been in the U.K. for thirteen weeks running a series of workshops around the country. I call them "Healing with Energies". They are two-day affairs where I attune people into Reiki and Seichim mastery for a nominal fee.' Ted hesitated, expecting Bob to turn away from such a fringe topic. 'And also it is a way that I can promote my books.' To Ted's surprise, Bob actually seemed more interested.

'I imagine they were a great success.'

'On the contrary,' Ted complained. The bitterness in his voice showed.

Bob, unfazed, listened to the story of the tour. When Ted finished Bob laughed. 'Sounds like a brilliant success to me. How did you start running these workshops?'

'I ran the first "Healing with Energies" workshop because I needed the money. In my daytime disguise, I worked for a Canadian-owned software development company as their business development manager. Frankly, I didn't like it. I was a published author, a fact that didn't impress my bank manager, and I was trying to write a stage play. My job at Octagon was purely nine to five and for the dollars. I was good at business development yet at Octagon I lost it. One didn't have to be psychic to know that eventually the writing describing my demise was on the wall.' Ted paused as the memories trickled back.

'Ted, surely it wasn't all bad?' Bob prodded.

'I can't make sense of that time,' Ted confided.

'Well, try and find the thread. People choose jobs as places where they can test out their theories about who they are. Jobs, or other facets of life, are the arenas where we can create in the physical world. They are places where we can prove to ourselves who we are. That's part of the Thread Theory,' Bob continued.

Ted thought for a moment. 'Places to prove who I am? The Octagon experience proved who I was not!'

'There you are, then,' Bob declared triumphantly. Ted, on the other hand, was confused. His face showed it. 'Go on then, continue with the story,' Bob prompted.

'I suppose all was not lost at Octagon. The company hired a part-time bookkeeper and office manager. Octagon had a knack of hiring people who didn't want to work there. "Only in it for the money" could well have been the company's motto. Even the Canadian managing director and his wife were en-route to their silent dream. More than once they admitted after the Friday ritual tequila toast, that they were only working at

Octagon to save enough money to buy a small boutique bed and breakfast in Spain. Perhaps energy attracts energy. Roger and Molly, who introduced me to Octagon, were former employees. Roger, the now ex-business development manager, and Molly, the ex-book keeper, office manager and publicist. Roger and Molly were husband and wife whose love was not for the computer industry. Rather it was to open their own breeding kennel for pit bull terriers. Fortunately for me, because I got Roger's job, and fortunately for Craig, who slipped into Molly's role.

'Not surprisingly, Craig only took the part-time job for the money. Coincidentally, he too was a budding playwright. Octagon was a small company in Australia with most of its technical people working out on our clients' sites. Hence, Craig and I had many meaningful discussions about writing. I had been at Octagon for about six months when Craig sauntered over to my workstation. "Ted, ma boy," the fifty-three year old Canadian drawled. "We've gotta have a heart-to-heart, you and me. No holds barred and straightshootin'."

I felt honoured that Craig wanted to confide in me and told him so. "Hell, no, Ted! I don't want to talk about me. It's about you." I looked into his eyes and could see a hesitation that soon steeled into determination. "Ted, I've watched you for three months now and I can no longer bear to watch your soul die. You've gotta leave this confounded place before you kill it completely. Your soul's sick, man, and you've gotta feed it. Stop doin' this to yaself."

'As he was talking, my mind flicked back six months prior. I worked as a headhunter in a friend's recruitment practice. I took that job for the money as well. I had been a successful headhunter in the eighties before I chucked it in to sell computers. So it was like coming home to RW & A. I think I was there about six months when Rachael called me into her office.

'"Ted, I just can't stand it," she blurted out.

'"Rachael, I know I am taking longer to get on my feet —"

'"It's not that, Ted," she interrupted. "I just can't bare to see you so miserable. This is not for you anymore, your spirit's not in it and it's killing your soul." Rachael then promptly sacked me.'

Ted paused momentarily. His eyes clouded over with a touch of confused sadness.

'There's something else inside you, Ted. Do you want to tell me what it is?' Bob asked.

'Oh, it's nothing really, just a thought.' The chess game was back on.

'Sometimes it's the nothings that guide us to the threads. Ted, tell me what the nothing is.' By pushing hard, Bob was exposing his king's bishop. It was a risky move. Yet Bob felt that the risk was necessary. Silence. Bob could see Ted collecting his thoughts. Now the pregnant pause was no longer a sales ploy. It was a silence that reached deep into the void.

'Ted!' Bob nudged.

'I am just trying to get my words around the thought.' Ted began: 'I can't see how it is relevant here yet I suppose it won't hurt to tell you. The interesting thing was that after Rachael sacked me she then insisted that because I had not performed to her expectation that somehow I had let her down.'

'That's preposterous, Ted. Owners of businesses always take risk on their staff. They would happily take the profit you generated. Equally they should accept the loss. That's business. Surely you explained that to her!'

Ted winced. 'Actually, no. I felt so guilty not living up to her expectations that I promised to pay back my salary. Even now she is chasing me for it.'

'Does that happen often?' Bob moved his attack bishop away to a less threatening position.

'All the time. I just hate confrontation, yet I seem to be the master at creating it. Then when it happens I just lie down and let the steamroller run over me.'

Bob slowly pushed forward again. 'Ted? When do these confrontations occur?'

'They've happened most of my life. My mother tells me that as a child I was so stubborn that I would never back down. Sometimes she said my father would spank me so hard that she thought I would turn blue. I can't remember any of it, though. All I can remember was the tactic after that.'

'Oh?'

'When I stubbornly stood my ground they would shut me in the laundry. It was a room built onto the back veranda.'

'How did you react to that?' Bob gently nudged.

'I hated it. Mum says that it worked like a charm until....' Ted's eyes changed again. Sadness left and a twinkle of defiance could be seen in the corner of his eyes. He smiled triumphantly. 'On one occasion when they locked me in, I plugged the wash basin and turned the taps on full bore. They had to let me out when they saw water gushing from under the door. After that we reached an understanding.'

Bob noticed the way Ted changed as he told the story. It appeared to Bob that Ted felt he was truly himself when he turned the tap on. Ted's energy lifted at that point. He became animated, alive and charged with life. 'Why did your parents punish you?'

'Because I loved to tell stories. Because of their religious beliefs stories were untruths. They defined stories as lies. Therefore, that made telling stories sinful. They were trying to save me, I guess.' Ted regained his conservative stance, then moved his queen's knight into attack. 'What has this got to do with the Thread Theory?' he demanded.

Bob moved a pawn to the rescue. He shrugged his shoulders. 'Did you like telling stories?'

'Must have,' Ted responded. 'Mum told me after I published my first book that she always knew I was a writer. I was amazed. I only decided to write after I turned forty. She never told me. I asked her why not.'

'She replied?' Bob urged, now fully enthralled.

'She told me that she and my father discussed it and decided not to promote it because there was no money in it.' That look came back into Ted's eyes.

'What? What is it, Ted?'

'A thought just struck me. Jill, my first publisher, always told me that whenever I complained that my books weren't selling quick enough, "When will you learn that there is no money in writing!". I've even chosen my mother as a publisher! I remember once when Jill told me that, I was reading a newspaper. I glanced down at an article about Stephen King. He had just signed a deal for two manuscripts unwritten for $77 million. I remember thinking that he obviously had a different mother.'

'Be careful not to get entangled in the threads of the story, Ted. If you do, it will halt you in your tracks and you will take a long time to disentangle yourself from it,' Bob cautioned. Bob could see a pattern forming. To him the message was clear. Ted could survive in this world, but survival was not enough for him. 'Ted, you will never rest until you find out how to nurture your soul,' Bob counselled.

Ted looked at Bob. 'Do you think that I can kill my soul?'

'I am not a theologian, Ted. Yet I do know that you can heal it. In order to do that you first must find what your soul wants to express in this lifetime.'

'How do I do that?' Ted's question had a hopeless ring to it.

'Usually your soul tells you when you are young. Not in a direct vocal way.'

'No voices booming from the heavens then,' Ted chuckled.

'It's more subtle than that, Ted. It usually manifests as a daydream. Something that we dream we would like to be yet we don't believe that we are good enough to do it. The dream keeps rising into our thoughts and if we haven't caught it by the time we are forty, then we usually go into crisis until we do....'

Ted interrupted. 'Sure, I had a dream, realised what I wanted to do when I turned forty. I was single then. Bob, it's easy to sacrifice to achieve your dreams when you are single. Yet soon after I realised what I wanted to do I fell in love with Marianne. Shortly afterwards, we were living together with her three boys. Then things changed. It's okay to sacrifice myself for my cause, yet how do I ask those that I love and who depend on me to sacrifice their goals, dreams and ambitions for mine?'

'I don't understand.' Bob pushed forward. 'How did you get into the healing business if you wanted to write?'

'When I was working at RW & A a friend introduced me to Heather Christensen, who attuned me to master status of the Reiki and Seichim models of healing. So, thinking of ways to earn extra money, I got the notion to run a "Healing with Energies" weekend in Newcastle.'

'Newcastle?' Bob asked.

Ted continued. 'It's a large urban town two hours north of Sydney. I had, in the past, run psychic development classes in the region so had a base of clients to work off. In fact, it was through this group that I rekindled my interest in Reiki. I received Reiki First and Second Degree attunements many years before I developed as a spiritual healer. Frankly neither modality felt energetically different, only the form that the healing was cloaked in. The common thread in my Newcastle psychic classes was that most students had been attuned to Reiki First Degree, with at least half being attuned to Reiki Second Degree. As more became involved in Reiki Second Degree, several people began to spontaneously channel. That is, spirit intelligence would directly speak through them. This interested me at first because there appeared to be a psychic dimension to Reiki that was never spoken about. I think this was because a significant proportion of Reiki masters are not psychically developed, nor competent psychic mediums. Often, when one develops as a psychic, it is difficult initially to distinguish between a spirit being or one's alter ego. Then there is the problem of identifying credible spirit beings and those just wanting to be heard. Mother Mary seemed to be speaking regularly through several Reiki Second Degree initiates. I noticed that coincidentally they were reading a book called *Messages from Mary*. The other thing that I noticed was that the channels were becoming physically unhealthy and energy drained. Something was out of balance and I thought I knew what.

'Genuinely wanting to help, I requested a meeting with their Reiki master. She granted me an audience. I suggested to her that perhaps her Reiki Second Degree students could benefit from an introductory psychic class to help them deal with the energies. Sylvia looked at me without a sign of emotion. My Psychic 101 suggestion seemed to have sailed right past her and out of the window.

'"I am happy to do it for free," I continued, thinking that she may have a thought that I was after her business.

She told me that she did not see any problems; that the reactions I had witnessed were the result of the symbols being programmed into them. That these symbols open the gateway between the conscious and subconscious minds. She told me that the students would just have to learn to deal with the fall out, and that a good support team was ready.

"Are they aware at the time of the attunements that this is what you are doing to them?" I asked.

Sylvia said they were not, and declared that only masters had the secret knowledge, and that not everyone could have access to the sacred symbols. I remember sitting in her consulting rooms stunned. She thanked me for coming, but told me that I could be of no help in the workshop.

'At the time I couldn't take the discussion further because I didn't know what the secret symbols were. The keys to unlock the Holy Grail. Perhaps my curiosity was sparked that day and remained in a deep recess of my mind waiting for an opportunity, like Heather Christensen, to come along. Maybe it was my meeting with Sylvia that prepared the soil for me to want to pay

$6500 to satisfy my curiosity about the secret symbols.' Ted stopped. He seemed to have lost the thread of what he was saying and why he was saying it. 'Bob, do you really want to hear these ramblings about my personal experiences?'

Bob, realising that Ted's resolve was spent, looked at his watch. 'Perhaps we should pause here. I can smell dinner coming. Just understand that in the tapestry of your life's story is stitched the picture of your drive to self-mastery. All parts of your life, whether you like them or not, are important sub-themes to the main story-line.'

The two separated energetically. Each was thinking about the Thread Theory. For Bob there was a sense of amazement about the theory. He could see how it worked throughout his life. Yet it always puzzled him when he tried to unravel the 'How did it work so perfectly?' tangle.

Ted, on the other hand, sunk back into depression. He wondered why he had created the story that he was embroiled in. 'I must be a lousy creator,' he said quietly to himself as the stewardess placed his meal on the tray in front of him.

Sleep came easily after the meal. Perhaps it had something to do with the double whisky he ordered with it. Nevertheless, Ted drifted into the half-world of dreams. Since childhood he had a recurring dream. He had explored it from most psycho-pathological angles yet still the dream persisted. It usually appeared when he was wondering just what was his purpose in life. He believed that he must have a purpose to find fulfilment. Therefore, the truth that was ever so elusive for Ted was that he was actually seeking self-fulfilment. The purpose was just the vehicle that transported him to it. Whether it was the whisky this time or a spirit of a higher source didn't matter because Ted was walking through an uninhabited land.

In this dream, Jeremy was his guide and master. No one knew how old Jeremy was because he had always been there. Some speculated that he was at least 800 years of age. Jeremy had convinced Ted to walk from a village on the plains to a village five days away at the foot of a mountain range. They packed enough supplies for the march with an extra day's surplus. Two days into the march the rains came. A sub-tropical downpour that transformed the walking track into the bottom of a riverbed that was now five foot beneath the frothing surface. Ted and Jeremy were forced to camp beside the raging torrent for three days. Their supplies ran out and they were threatened with starvation. On the sixth day the rain stopped.

'Jeremy,' Ted said, wanting a warm meal that only the village could supply. 'Let's get moving. C'mon!'

Jeremy looked at Ted and replied lazily: 'I would prefer to wait until the path dries out. It's too slippery at the moment. Let's give it another day'.

Ted looked at Jeremy in amazement. 'If we don't make a start we will starve out here!'

'Is that all you are worried about?' Jeremy asked.

'Isn't starving enough?' Ted lost his patience.

Jeremy looked at Ted with the patience of a thousand saints. In Ted's dream this patient, all-knowing look haunted him. 'Ted, if it is only food you want then all we have to do is plant some wheat.' Jeremy held out his left hand and wheat grains appeared in his palm. 'Then all we have to do is to plant them.' Jeremy bent down to a patch of wet dirt and planted the seeds. 'Now we should ask them to grow.' There, as it always was, in front of Ted's dreamy eyes the wheat began to grow until it ripened. 'Let's harvest it now. We can make a meal out of it and bake a loaf of bread,' Jeremy instructed.

Ted did exactly that. He baked a loaf on the campfire. As he was eating the warm, doughy feast he remarked, 'Jeremy, you always amaze me. I don't know why I ever doubt you. When it comes to miracles ...'

Jeremy held up his hand to stop Ted. '"Miracle", Ted! Can't you see how limited your thinking is? All I gave you was a process because that is what you wanted. Remember that creation is about manifesting what you focus on. If it was bread that you wanted …' And with that Jeremy produced loaves of bread from nowhere.

The dream ended with, 'Ouch!'. This time it was Bob returning to his seat after a stroll around the cabin. 'Sorry,' Bob apologised. Ted stretched. 'Bob, does focusing on the process have anything to do with your thread theory?' Bob looked at Ted with empathy. 'I always find that a Bloody Mary sits better with me than whisky when I fly.'

Chapter 8

The Reiki Analogy

'In the beginning was … Reiki.' Actually, I can't really confirm how old Reiki is. Reiki masters, however, say that it is ancient. In modern times, Mikao Usui, a Japanese, claimed to have rediscovered it. Whether he did or not, I suggest, does not matter. What does matter is that, intrinsic within the living world there is a force or energy that binds divergent energies together in an harmonious life-giving way.

This book is a thesis on health. Its underlying premise is the assumption that we are whole and that the process of healing is a process of remembering who we are. Now, if we accept that premise then it follows that by being whole, we are also perfect. That's a more challenging statement because wholeness and perfection are considered states and exist in the realms of thought which we think of as *I am*.

If *we are* or *I am* then healing is a process of moving into I AM consciousness. Sounds simple, but it isn't when you are living in a state of chronic illness. I remember when I had gallstones. For years, I tried to heal myself. I tried emotional healing, naturopathic cleanses, energetic healing and Reiki. Nothing worked. I vividly remember lying on my bed writhing in agony during an attack crying out, 'I am supposed to be a healer yet I can't heal myself!'. In the middle of a gall bladder attack the bliss of the I AM state seems as attainable as an ant jumping over Mt Everest in a single bound.

In this chapter, the word 'state' is used frequently. A person may be in a healthy state. Perhaps you are in a blissful state. When someone is said to be 'all in a tizzy' we commonly describe that person as being in a state. There are also two words associated with each other: 'being' and 'state'. It appears that when we are in a certain *state* we limit ourselves to the characteristics of that state.

81

Therefore, if I am in a happy state, it is impossible for me to be in a sad state at the same time. People say that we cannot be in different places at the same time. This also applies to states. In a sense when I am in a happy state, I am also *being* happy. Note that I am not *doing* happy. Hence, we talk about states of being. How do I know when I am in a state? Because when I *am* in a state ... whoops, there it is again. When I am in a state of happiness then I usually say that I am happy. Therefore, the 'I am' that is commonly spoken about as describing God is actually verbal shorthand to let people know what state I am in.

So what about the *doing* side of life? I suggest that we move from one state to another by the act of *doing* something. This doing something is an activity. A collection of activities is called a process. People say that we create karma by doing something. 'Karma' is a word that describes what happens to a state around us after we start to do something in that state. Karma, then, is the process of changing states through action. Is your head hurting yet? Mine is, and I suspect that it is going to get worse before the end of the chapter.

If I am healed then I exist in a state of wholeness. If I am ill then I exist in a state of illness. A premise about states is that they are. Therefore, the suggestion hangs over us that to exist in a state is to do nothing. It is just to *be*. The masters, people say, exist in a state of being. Compare this to the karmic model of cause and effect. The karmic model implies activity, or movement between inactive states. Whereas the wholeness model implies ... well, is sitting on a cloud playing a harp getting close? Boring! It was thinking about the concept that prompted me to do something. So I wrote a stage play. It's called *What Turns Me On*. The play explores what could happen if familiarity breeds contempt, and God is so familiar with perfection (and being whole) that He or She loses it completely. Is this when we become vulnerable to the serpent's suggestion?

'Would you like to have more knowledge than you have now?' The snake is cunning in a cuddly sort of way. It knows that we are whole so it can't give us more wholeness unless it creates an illusion. An illusion that we are *not* whole or we are incomplete.

The snake achieves this by focusing us on our different states and then suggesting to us that these differences somehow make us incomplete and, you guessed it, no longer whole. When Adam and Eve fell for the serpent's suggestion and they ate the fruit, immediately they noticed they were naked. The Bible says that they saw their nakedness, were ashamed and hid. How times have changed! Christianity's first mythological archetypes saw they were naked and hid. Hence, the fashion industry evolved. Today the fashion industry tries to enhance the naked form by designing clothes that hint at our nakedness without actually showing 100 per cent bare flesh.

Consider the irony here. Seductive fashion is a cleverly designed *cover-up*! The fashion industry hints at the serpent's original promise, 'I can show you more than you can see now'. Yet, the fashion industry has a distinct problem. If the promises to show all become reality then the fashion industry will die because no one will wear any clothes! Adam and Eve noticed that they were different and I suggest that instead of celebrating their differences they became ashamed of them. Perhaps somewhere inherent within them dwelled a social conformity gene. Perhaps the knowledge that the serpent wanted to impart to Adam and Eve was that, although we are one, we manifest selected God characteristics in each incarnation. Perhaps the serpent wanted to reveal to Adam and Eve the futility of losing oneself in a group sense of conformity. What you will read next is central to the point I want to make throughout this book.

We need to consider some potentially blasphemous suggestions. If God is *all* then the serpent, by definition, is a part of God. Perhaps the serpent represents God's shadow side. If the serpent is a part of God then it was God in the tree talking with a serpent attitude. The New English version of the Bible says in Genesis Chapter 3:4 and 5 (the serpent is talking to Eve about the consequences of eating the fruit): 'You will not surely die,' the serpent said to the woman. 'For God knows that when you eat of it your eyes will be opened and you will be like God, knowing good and evil.'

Well, the serpent was wrong because Adam and Eve died — or was he? Let's read on to Verse 22: 'And the Lord God said about Adam: "The *man has now become like one of us*, knowing good and evil. He must not be allowed to reach out his hand and take also from the tree of life and eat and live forever".' Irony was alive and well before William Shakespeare. In this parable, God, the creator of everything including Adam and Eve, when faced with his creations being like him, kicked them out of the God club. God sure was a jealous God! Perhaps this story reflects ingrained aspects of humanity as well as the nature of God.

We strive for perfection. We strive for nirvana or heaven, whatever we believe to be the infinite state of wholeness. Yet, when we get there, we can't face the suggestion that others can also reach wholeness *in their own way*. Therefore, we become territorial and create entry conditions to stop people living in the same state as us. We do this in a most sinister and insidious manner. We simply suggest that they can't enter through the gates of heaven unless they are exactly like us. That is, we place conditions on them so that they behave the same way, talk the same way, believe the same things we believe and so on. So we call ourselves 'masters' and establish the myth that, because we have entered the forest, we can teach others to walk along the pathways that we have created. If we push this line of thought then we become people who exploit another's need to conform, rather than celebrating that people can exist in wholeness even though they reside in different states.

Sometime in our evolution, we developed a need to be the same. Do the same things. Practise the same techniques and so on. Granted, we do allow ourselves some latitude yet it is still in the mould we deem to be acceptable.

In *What Turns Me On*, I explore the humorous paradoxes between the *being states* and the *doing states*. In the play, God becomes totally lost and comes to earth half-remembering who he is. He knows he can create anything, be anything and do anything so adopts the personality of a schizophrenic. It's ironic really how we humans are forever trying to do something to find our bliss. The play is a romp between God who is lost and trying to rediscover bliss by being human and humans wanting to be gods by doing things that they see as special. Perhaps I should have called the play *Changing States*. I suggest that activity is merely a process of changing states. That conflict occurs when a god of one state cannot accept a god of another state. For example, if I am in a state of feeling unfulfilled and I want to be in a state of fulfilment, I must do something and create a bridge that I can travel across to leave a state of being unfulfilled to a fulfilled state.

For me, I believe that I will find fulfilment through writing and, indeed, I do — sometimes. The bridge that I need to create, in order to travel into my defined state of fulfilment, is a writing bridge. In other words, what I choose as my creative outlet in this lifetime acts as the bridge between the states of being unfulfilled and fulfilled.

What happens then when people ask me, 'Bruce, how do I create my own bliss?'.

'That's easy,' I reply. 'You must learn to write. It's so fulfilling.'

'But I can't write,' the questioner replies.

'Well, that's the only thing that is keeping you from being fulfilled.'

'Then will you teach me how to write, please? I want to be as fulfilled as you are. Please show me *exactly* how you do it. Then if I can just do it the same as you then I will get there!'

If I go along with this request, several things can happen concurrently. I could feel important. Clearly, I have something that another person does not. I am in a position of power because I can dictate what the other person should do to be like me, so I become deified and teach fulfilment to people by trying to create them in my own image. If the person accepts my story, then I have something of perceived value that this person doesn't have.

Since this is a commercial world, I can establish myself as the bliss expert and sell my services for a handsome profit. I can even suggest that because my road is a difficult one, we need to learn it in stages. Therefore, I can sell the bliss course by the module — Bliss 101, Bliss 201 and Bliss Mastery. The process could take years. I could establish a Bliss University offering degrees, diplomas and certificates in Bliss Management. Perhaps it would be a good marketing pitch to put my photograph on the qualification certificates and diplomas so people have a constant reminder of just how important it is in bliss realisation to be exactly like me.

However, there may be a person who has the audacity to think that life is already blissful. 'I didn't write to get there. I did it through music. People could really find their bliss just as I did by playing jazz guitar.' Therefore, a new Bliss School emerges. The problem that the second school has is that it needs its own identity. Here it comes again. It needs its own point of difference for people to conform to. Soon the new bliss school teaching jazz guitar rises in prominence. My student enrolments drop off and there are rumblings amongst my teaching staff that they would like to experience bliss the jazz-guitar way.

I am facing all sorts of fears. I am losing students. My revenue is falling. Yet, there is something more at stake than that. What happens if there is more bliss in playing jazz guitar than in writing? Have I wasted all my time on a creative pursuit that didn't have it all? I go on a retreat to re-think my marketing strategy. I need to keep business going because I have financially leveraged three investment industrial complexes. But, more importantly, my whole self-esteem has somehow become linked with teaching bliss realisation rather than actually living in the bliss state and writing. Somewhere along the way, I changed states without consciously creating the bridge! How do I get back to my bliss state? I have forgotten how to write, it's been so long. Perhaps I should investigate ancient teachings to find my heritage, to remember that I can write. What will I do?

Let's pause here to examine the Reiki story as it is traditionally told. I will summarise the events. (A more detailed account of the emergence of Reiki is contained in books in the Bibliography.) Essentially, when you attend a Reiki First Degree course you will have the following explained to you:

1. The founder of the Reiki System of hands-on healing was Mikao Usui.

2. He was a Japanese theologian teaching at the Doshisha University in Kyoto, Japan.

3. During a lecture, one of his students asked him how Jesus healed and when Usui could not answer the question he resigned and started his quest to find the answer.

4. His search took him to the United States of America where he studied theology at the University of Chicago Divinity School and he graduated from the doctoral program. Hence his title Dr Mikao Usui.

5. Although he gained academic credentials in the United States, he did not find the answer to the question of how Jesus healed.

6. He then travelled throughout Asia studying Sanskrit and Buddhist teachings.

7. Somewhere in his travels he discovered a set of Sanskrit symbols pertaining to healing. It is these symbols that the Reiki fraternity claim act as the keys that open the universal healing banks of energy.

8. After receiving (discovering) the symbols he went up a mountain where he fasted and prayed for an extensive period of time until he found the sequence that the symbols needed to be drawn in to evoke the energy.

9. It is this sequence of symbols that the Reiki fraternity calls an attunement. That is, to evoke the expression of universal healing energy within a person they need to undergo a series of attunements.

10. The story maintains that after Mikao Usui underwent this attunement process, his healing power was so strong that as he walked down from the mountains and through the villages people who came into his energy field who needed healing were healed.

Let us examine the traditional story and compare it to how a master teaches Reiki today. I suggest that when we realise the intrinsic steps in the process, we will find the universal formula for self-healing and becoming a master.

STEP 1 — *The Realisation of Lack*
The question asked of Mikao Usui was a question that he could not answer. Because of this, he suspected that there might be another state he wanted to live in.

STEP 2 — *Creation of the Desire*
Mikao Usui wanted to find the answer to the question and hence move into the healing state. This may sound trite, but this is where we begin whenever we seek change. Mikao Usui wanted to find the answer. In other words, it was through his perceived state of lack — the inability to answer the question — that he created the desire to find the answer. It is enough here to note that all creations begin with the acknowledgment that the person (creator) wants something that they perceive they don't have. This acknowledgment of lack creates the desire to find what will satisfy it.

STEP 3 — *Intending to do Something About It*
When the desire became intense enough, Mikao Usui intended
to do something about it. So far, the bridging process looks
something like this:

> RECOGNITION OF LACK leads to the
> DESIRE TO SATISFY THE LACK, which leads to the
> INTENTION TO SATISFY THE LACK …

How many times have you perceived a lack in your life and felt
that you were somehow inadequate? It is at this stage that people
decide to either create their way out of the lack or to feel a failure. If
acceptance of the latter happens then the creative bridge collapses
through lack of use. Another way to explain this is to view our
environment as a pool of water. At one end of the pool, a river feeds
the pool and at the other end, a river leaves the pool. The water is
able to flow through the pool and it remains clean, clear and healthy.

If the creator of the water system forgets to maintain the outlet
to the river leaving the pool and focuses only on the pool, then
the river leading from the pool may dam up. Although outward flow
stops, the feeding river still pushes its desires into the pool, filling it
with increasingly unfulfilled desires. The mounting pressures of the
water breaks the banks of the pool and floods the surrounding
areas, swamping their purposes until the pool becomes a backwater.
In Australia, we call these backwaters billabongs. These billabongs
are stagnant bodies of water that become undrinkable, unusable
and a breeding place for mosquitoes, flies, bacteria and disease.

The alternative is to view the creation of lack in your life with
passionate excitement. Why? Because it is the first sign of pressure
that the seed (you) wants to create. Mikao Usui listened to this urge
and *intended* to do something about it.

STEP 4 — *Acting on Intention*
Mikao Usui, after realising Steps 1, 2 and 3 as positive creative energy
swells, did something about it. Note that the creative process weaves

its way through the inner world and the outer world. Steps 1, 2 and 3 all occur within the organism (that's you and me!). This is the process. I realise that I do not have something that I believe will take me to my bliss state (deficit need). I want to satisfy my deficit needs (desire). I decide to do something to satisfy my desire (intention).

A part of my life's work is to inspire people to act on their creative desires. Therefore, I study creative people. When I first met Katrina, I didn't know how to recognise the creative process. A part of her talents is that she is an artist. At times I remember feeling her discontent. She would be touchy, anxious, intolerant and generally on edge. I thought that it was a reaction towards me. How wrong I was! Her agitation would last for a while and then peace would settle over the house. I revelled in the peace until I realised that the only reason that it was peaceful was that Katrina had disappeared. She would disappear into her studio to paint. Now that I can recognise creative unrest, I see it everywhere. It even works within myself. I get edgy, become almost unbearable until I realise that I am about to write something new — perhaps a poem, a story concept, a business strategy. In my opinion, this is how creativity begins. It begins through a state of dis-ease.

Ironically, people fight these feelings of dis-ease as if they have done something wrong. They seek counselling, therapy, go on drugs, when all that needs to happen is for them to do something to express their creative desires. My belief is that illness is purely the indicator, that our personality has forgotten that it is the doer in the creative process. Instead of focusing energy on creating the soul's desires it expends its energy in searching for what it perceives to be the soul's desire through inappropriate activities.

Imagine that the soul is a bank manager. For this analogy, I ask that you assume the role of the bank manager. A potential borrower, a friend, asks to borrow money from your bank. Pat, your friend, tells you that he has found his life's purpose. After years of meditation, counselling and herbal remedies, Pat realises that he wants to become a gourmet chef. What is more, he wants to open a chain of quality health restaurants where people can be entertained during their meals by inspirational speakers.

You look into Pat's eyes and see his enthusiasm. Your intuition tells you that this indeed is Pat's mission in life. You know that he will realise his dreams. You want to help Pat. Pat tells you that the only obstacle in his path is funding. Because you have graduated from Lending School, you know that intuition is not enough. You were taught in Assessing Risk 101 that you need more than your intuition. 'Pat,' you say. 'I feel you will be successful. Drop in your business plan and if it looks good then I will lend you the money that you need.' Pat in fact produces a business plan from his back pocket. You look at the plan. It impresses you. You know that Pat has the energy to implement the plan and to succeed.

You lend Pat all of the $250,000 that he asks for and you tell him just to pay it back when he is successful. Time is not the issue here. You trust that Pat's plans will work. Pat leaves happy and you relax back in your chair knowing you have helped a person toward creating a dream. Time passes. You don't hear from Pat. That's okay, he's probably busy being successful. More time passes. You are with your family at the beach, and you see Pat and his family lunching at a seaside cafe. Naturally, the reunion is pleasant. 'How is the project going, Pat?' you ask.

'Great,' replies Pat. 'I have been planning to call you. I underestimated the capital I needed.'

You interrupt excitedly, knowing that his plans are succeeding. 'I can lend you another $250,000 if that helps.'

Pat looks relieved. 'Oh. I didn't want that much, but if it's on offer I could use it.' You tell Pat to drop into the bank on Monday and you will arrange the funds transfer.

So it's off to the beach and as you are crossing the road your daughter says: 'Pat must really be successful. I love his new Mercedes sports car!'. You nod yes and find a spot on the sand. The weeks pass and you hear snippets of Pat's success from friends. He has moved into a bigger house. He looked good after his holidays to Europe, although you do think it strange that he is back at his old job. Every so often, you see him on the golf course. He waves across to you, yet now you feel something is just not right. Then, one Friday before closing time, the telephone rings.

PAT: Hi there, have I caught you at an awkward time?

YOU: No Pat, I was just finishing for the day. How is it going?

PAT: Well, I have a problem. I wonder if you can help.

YOU: Sure, I have some time next Wednesday, perhaps we could meet then —

PAT: Actually, it's more important than that. I have a cash flow problem now. What with running the family, trying to satisfy all their needs, I haven't had the time I needed to get the project going.

YOU: Going! Pat I thought it was really powering along.

PAT: Can we get to that in a minute? I need $5000 by Monday, otherwise my car will be repossessed and the house mortgage will go into default.

YOU: Well, I can lend you more, Pat (*You have an infinite money supply*). However, before I do, I will need to see just what stage you are at in your business plan.

PAT: (*Silence for what seems an eternity*) Actually, I haven't finished the pilot study. So many things have got in my way. I had to go on holidays. I went back to my old job to earn more so I could repay you.

Yet the more I earned the more I got into debt.
You have to help me.

Let's stop the play there. How do you feel? Will you lend Pat more money? I know what I would do. I'd cut my losses as much for him as for me. I would stop the flow of money because Pat is not using the money to create his brilliance.

I believe our soul is the bank manager to the universal life-giving creative energy bank. It can generate infinite supplies of energy at will. Granted, it does not create money, as we know it, yet it does supply our personality (Pat) with the necessary energy to achieve its life's purpose or life's mission. There are times in our lives where our personalities are so distracted in the karmic state that we lose sight of the soul's goals and use up all its energy. My belief is that when our personalities stray too far from the soul's purpose then the soul cuts off the energy supply to the physical machine that is the vehicle of doing.

The question is: how can we resume the energy flow when we are lost and no longer know what our purpose is? The answer, I believe, is through intent with activity. The story of Mikao Usui illustrates this. He went in search of his Holy Grail to find the answer to the question of how Jesus healed. This searching is the step that guarantees that you will find the Grail. A much-quoted verse in the Bible is: 'Ask and ye shall receive'. Yet, the answers don't always come in easily recognisable forms. Rather, they tend to come cloaked in the robes of our socioeconomic upbringing. I am an Australian and I speak only English. It would be of no value to me if I heard or read the answer to my Holy Grail question in a language other than English. We receive truth in our individual contexts.

Dr Mikao Usui was Japanese. He studied Eastern philosophies and traditions. Therefore, it makes sense to me that he discovered his truth — 'How did Jesus do healings?'— in an Eastern tongue, from his cultural context. Reiki teaching centres on the signing of

Eastern symbols in various sequences. This action of signing symbols is another form of communication. There are five basic Reiki symbols. (For a more detailed discussion of these symbols, I suggest you read Diane Stein's wonderful book on Reiki called *Essential Reiki*.) Please note that traditional Reiki masters will probably insist that you remember these symbols and not disclose them to anyone. Therefore, when you sign them you should make sure that no one sees you doing it. I have heard Reiki masters suggest that the practitioner sign the symbols on the upper palate of the mouth using the tip of the tongue.

CHO-KU-REI

Reiki masters claim that the signing of the CHO-KU-REI increases your ability to access and transmit Reiki energy to your clients. They call it the power symbol. Healers sign the CHO-KU-REI over problem areas in an attempt to speed up the healing. They draw the symbol over medicines, foods, and I have even seen the sign drawn on people's chequebooks. It is a symbol that Reiki practitioners claim will enhance and speed up good fortune.

HON-SHA-ZE-SHO-NEN

HON-SHA-ZE-SHO-NEN is used to send healing distantly. Conventional Reiki healing occurs when the Reiki practitioner either touches the client or places the hands no more than a couple of inches away from the skin. They sign the HON-SHA-ZE-SHO-NEN over an image (either photographic or imagined) of the client, and they believe this enables the energy to travel across large distances.

SEI-HE-KI

The SEI-HE-KI promotes emotional healing, purification and protection. They say that it is the guiding light to the subconscious and will awaken the god/goddess within. Practitioners use the SEI-HE-KI to protect open wounds from infection. They sign it around their children to keep them safe. I have a friend who signs it over the parking meter to protect him from you know who!

TAM-A-RA-SHA

Reiki masters sometimes replace the TAM-A-RA-SHA with a lightning-bolt-type symbol called the RAKU. (I haven't shown the RAKU in this text, as it wasn't a symbol that I learnt. You can find it in Diane Stein's book.) Reiki masters use the TAM-A-RA-SHA in attunements, and when they want to unify the physical, emotional, intellectual and spiritual states. They use this as a balancing symbol.

DAI-KO-MIO

The DAI-KO-MIO is the big daddy of the Reiki symbols. It is the master symbol. It is used in all attunements to evoke Reiki energy and make Reiki First and Second Degree practitioners as well as Reiki masters. It is the most secret symbol. It is the one upon which all other Reiki symbols rest. The symbol illustrated here is just one version of it. Diane Stein notes several variations of the DAI-KO-MIO. In my travels, I have come across at least twelve variations of the DAI-KO-MIO taught as the master symbol.

What is the intrinsic power of these symbols? I believe that they have no power of their own. My view is that a symbol is a visual expression of our intention. It is a communicative device. As you go about your daily life you encounter many symbols. There are traffic signals denoting stop, proceed with caution, walk, don't walk, no parking and metered parking. These are purely visual expressions of our intention to communicate a standard message. Every letter in the alphabet also denotes the intention to visually communicate something. Words are therefore the signing of symbols (letters) in certain sequences. Now, let's look at the stated assumptions of Reiki.

1. The symbols they use are sacred and therefore Reiki masters should only initiate those into the Reiki fraternity who will use them responsibly.

2. Ditto with the sequencing of these symbols.

3. That the signing of these sequenced symbols (called attunements) can evoke the healing energies of the universe.

4. Reiki practitioners and masters must sign the symbols exactly the same way as first discovered by Usui to retain their purity and integrity.

5. Masters who are direct descendants in the Usui lineage are the only ones qualified, authorised and sanctified to make more masters or to teach the craft.

So far, I have given you the traditional Reiki philosophy. Now, here we go on a roller-coaster ride. I ask that you fasten your seatbelts and, as we run through the circuit, try to see the similarities in all facets of your life.

Reiki teaches seven levels or degrees. Level One, or First Degree, is the entry level. It is the first step up the ladder to perfection. It is the step nearest the ground. This is the most commonly sought-after Reiki qualification because once candidates have completed this level they are capable of practising as Reiki hands-on healers. That means they can deliver healing energy to a person via their hands. Reiki First Degree is taught over two days. During the workshops, Reiki masters teach the twelve standard Reiki hand positions. They explain the notion of hands-on healing, give students plenty of practice and, during the course of the weekend, the Reiki master will attune them into the Reiki energy.

There are usually four attunements. Each person receives two attunements on the first day and two on the second. The Reiki master will ask each student to nominate a power hand. It is the hand they want the energy to run through the strongest. It is not until the final attunement that the healing energy is fixed forever in your hands.

Why did I ask you to fasten your seatbelts? You may have noticed that since reading this book your hands have been tingling, getting hotter than usual, cooler than usual or just experiencing a different sensation. I am now going to list the four attunements. As you read them and examine them, you may feel an energy shift in your hands. Naturally Reiki and Seichim colleagues take exception to me revealing this information.

Well, here goes! The following is the complete attunements and instructions on how to attune people (including yourself) into Reiki First Degree.

REIKI 1st DEGREE

1st Attunement

STEPS

1 Stand behind initiate and put
   your hands on their shoulders

then

2 Sign TAM-A-RA-SHA three times

then

3 Sign CHO-KU-REI once, saying its
   name three times in your mind

then

4 Sign DAI-KO-MIO once

then

5 Sign CHO-KU-REI once, saying its
   name three times in your mind

then

6 Sign HON-SHA-ZE-SHO-NEN once

then

7 Sign CHO-KU-REI once, saying its
   name three times in your mind

then

8 Place your hands on top of initiate's
   neck and allow energy to flow in

then

    9   Walk to front of initiate and ask them
to raise their hand to prayer position

then

   10   Sign CHO-KU-REI once each to crown,
heart and throat; say name in your
mind three times for each sign

then

   11   Take initiate's hands and visualise
TAM-A-RA-SHA in palm of each hand

then

   12   Sign CHO-KU-REI once each to crown,
heart and throat; say name in your
mind three times for each sign

then

   13   Blow puff of breath to crown, heart, throat

then

   14   Sign CHO-KU-REI once each to crown,
heart and throat; say name in your
mind three times for each sign

then

   15   Advise initiate attunement is complete

REIKI 1st DEGREE

2nd Attunement

STEPS

1   Stand behind initiate and put your
     hands on their forehead

then

2   Sign TAM-A-RA-SHA three times

then

3   Sign CHO-KU-REI once, saying its
     name three times in your mind

then

4   Sign DAI-KO-MIO once

then

5   Sign CHO-KU-REI once, saying
     its name three times in your mind

then

6   Sign HON-SHA-ZE-SHO-NEN once

then

7   Sign CHO-KU-REI once, saying its
     name three times in your mind

then

8   Place your thumbs at base of initiate's
     neck and allow energy to flow in

then

9   Walk to front of initiate and ask them
    to raise their hand to prayer position

then

10 Sign CHO-KU-REI once each to crown,
    heart and throat; say name in your
    mind three times for each sign

then

11 Take initiate's hands and visualise
    TAM-A-RA-SHA in palm of each hand

then

12 Sign CHO-KU-REI once each to crown,
    heart and throat; say name in your
    mind three times for each sign

then

13 Blow puff of breath to crown, heart, throat

then

14 Sign CHO-KU-REI once each to crown,
    heart and throat; say name in your
    mind three times for each sign

then

15 Advise initiate attunement is complete

REIKI 1st DEGREE

3rd Attunement

STEPS

1   Stand behind initiate and put your
    hands on their shoulders

then

2   Sign TAM-A-RA-SHA three times

then

3   Sign CHO-KU-REI once, saying its
    name three times in your mind

then

4   Sign DAI-KO-MIO once

then

5   Sign CHO-KU-REI once, saying its
    name three times in your mind

then

6   Sign HON-SHA-ZE-SHO-NEN once

then

7   Sign CHO-KU-REI once, saying its
    name three times in your mind

then

8   Place your hands at base of initiate's
    neck and allow energy to flow in

then

9 Walk to front of initiate and ask them to raise their hand to prayer position

then

10 Sign CHO-KU-REI once each to crown, heart and throat; say name in your mind three times for each sign

then

11 Take initiate's hands and visualise TAM-A-RA-SHA in palm of each hand

then

12 Sign CHO-KU-REI once each to crown, heart and throat; say name in your mind three times for each sign

then

13 Blow puff of breath to crown, heart, throat

then

14 Sign CHO-KU-REI once each to crown, heart and throat; say name in your mind three times for each sign

then

15 Advise initiate attunement is complete

REIKI 1st DEGREE

4th Attunement

STEPS

1 Stand behind initiate and put your
hands on their head

then

2 Sign TAM-A-RA-SHA three times

then

3 Sign CHO-KU-REI once, saying its
name three times in your mind

then

4 Sign DAI-KO-MIO once

then

5 Sign CHO-KU-REI once, saying its
name three times in your mind

then

6 Sign HON-SHA-ZE-SHO-NEN once

then

7 Sign CHO-KU-REI once, saying its
name three times in your mind

then

8 Slide your left hand on back of initiate's
neck and place your right hand on the
crown to allow energy to flow in

then

9   Walk to front of initiate and ask them
     to raise their hand to prayer position

then

10   Sign CHO-KU-REI once each to crown,
     heart and throat; say name in your
     mind three times for each sign

then

11   Take initiate's hands and visualise
     TAM-A-RA-SHA in palm of each hand

then

12   Sign CHO-KU-REI once each to crown,
     heart and throat; say name in your
     mind three times for each sign

then

13   Blow puff of breath to crown, heart, throat

then

14   Sign CHO-KU-REI once each to crown,
     heart and throat; say name in your
     mind three times for each sign

then

15   Advise initiate attunement is complete

I almost forgot. Traditional Reiki First Degree workshops attune initiates in private with their eyes closed. Therefore, although they are attuned to the energy, they do not know consciously what was done to them. Therefore, they are unable to pass on the secrets. This presents a quandary for some people. If the attunements work and they are merely communicators of symbols then how does the communication transference occur?

Reiki masters explain that they implant the symbols into your aura. I guess they use long-life cosmic glue. In my practice, I often hear from concerned Reiki First Degree people who complain that the energy is wearing off. 'It doesn't feel as strong as it was at the attunements,' is a common comment. These people fear that the master who attuned them was not powerful enough to imbed the symbols permanently.

I believe that the reason why the attunements work in this blind situation is that the very act of sitting to receive the attunement is enough. Why? Because we are the absolute creators of our realities and we create via intention. Sitting for an attunement becomes an external expression of our intention. The initiate sits in the attunement room similar to the crippled man arriving at the place where the Nazarene was talking. The Reiki master performs a ritual that is intended to work. When these two intentions (yours by sitting and the master's by performing the ritual) resonate together then an alchemical moment occurs that invokes the memory within the initiate that they are a hands-on healer. The role of the Nazarene in the healing of the crippled man was to declare to him, 'you can do it'. The role of the Reiki master, is to declare that you can heal. Therefore, the Reiki master, by performing the ritual, is challenging you to take up your bed and walk.

Is it essential that an external person is involved in the process? I think not. There are numerous accounts of great healers who decided or discovered that they could be healers. Don't underestimate the power of the external environment. For any creative process to be complete, we need to express our internal intention externally. Therefore, to take up our beds and walk we need to do as the crippled man did. He walked. Therefore, to be a healer we need to express our intention by doing something. Simply by applying the healing in the external world.

Healers project themselves from the state of being a healer to the state of disease. Therefore, there is a communication highway established between the person receiving the healing (in the state of disease) and the healer (in the state of healing). The person's state of disease is their internal state. They heal by expressing their intention to heal and moving along the communication highway, via the energy provided by the hands-on healer, into the healer's state.

Let's put this into an everyday situation. When I had a toothache, I would hold off making an appointment with the dentist until the pain became unbearable. Quite often, after making an appointment, my toothache disappeared. Being a coward of sorts, I sometimes cancelled the appointment. Sure enough, the toothache returned. In this example, the toothache is my state of disease. The dentist's rooms are the state of 'tooth wellness'. The telephone line is my communication highway where I can express my intention to heal the toothache. When I make the call, I travel into the dentist's state and externally express my intention.

If the dentist decided to behave radically, he could take my call and declare, 'You are healed, go forth and chew vigorously on a block of chocolate'. If I decided to behave radically, I would follow his instructions, knowing the toothache healed. However, we are rational beings. We fear that this would not fix the toothache. Therefore, we attend the dental surgery to undergo a ritual so that the dentist can bestow renewed dental health onto our teeth. That is, he drills it, removes the decay and fills the cavity with a long-lasting and durable substance. He then declares that the tooth is fixed. We then take up our bed and leave the dental rooms healed. The healing process is just longer. Because we believe that we need to go to a dentist to fix a toothache, the first scenario will fail. We can only take up our bed (whatever the bed represents) when we know that we are whole. The healing process then is a process of remembering just that.

The Reiki First Degree attunement process inducts you into the 'How did Jesus heal?' school, but it leaves you ignorant of the answer. Don't despair; you do get a certificate to prove you don't know what you are doing.

The second level of Reiki or Reiki Second Degree is usually another two-day workshop that you can only participate in if you have completed Reiki First Degree. Some Reiki masters will only take you further if you have studied with them and no one else. In this workshop you will be told about three symbols, how to sign them, when to use them and what they do. These symbols are:

    1. CHO-KU-REI

    2. HON-SHA-ZE-SHO-NEN

    3. SEI-HE-KI

The Reiki master will require you to draw these symbols from memory exactly as Usui did in order to graduate. By the way, because the symbols are secret you will be prohibited from taking any written notes with you. Usually you burn them ceremoniously over a candle, although I have heard that some masters insist that their students eat the notes before leaving the workshop. I guess that way the student really integrates the symbols into their energy systems. All Second Degree initiates are asked not to divulge the secrets that they have learnt in the workshop, especially the symbols.

Reiki masters assert that the drawing or signing of the symbols exactly is a central point to performing Reiki competently.

Remember the William Blake saying? 'I must create a system or be
enslaved in another man's. I must not reason nor compare. My
business is to create.' I introduce symbols in my workshop by asking
a person from the audience to draw a dollar sign on a whiteboard.
Then I ask ten people to draw the same symbol on the whiteboard.
Do you know that every dollar sign is different? Every dollar sign is
a visual expression of our intention to communicate monetary
value. Although different, each symbol still conveys the same energy
of expression. From this quick experiment, we deduce that individuals
cannot exactly replicate what someone else has drawn. Yet, the
differences shown have no bearing on the communicative intent.

I also ask someone from the audience to draw ten separate
dollar signs on the white board. We quickly see that the person has
drawn each sign differently. So another deduction is that each
moment is different. People do not exactly replicate what they have
just done. This leads us to a quandary. If the same person cannot
replicate a previous signage then we can assume that the symbols
being purported as Dr Usui's are actually different from the original
symbols that he drew. My advice to you is to let go of the need to
replicate. It is more important that you focus your intent in creating
in the moment than trying to regress into a past state.

Moreover, there is one attunement given to each participant
during the Reiki Second Degree workshop. I just want to imbed
the symbols just taught to you into your hands so that you can
use them. Consider that what you believe is what you create. If
you believe that the attunement is actually imbedding the symbols
into the palms of your hands then I suggest that you refrain from
washing them until the cosmic glue sets. Yes I know I am a cynic.
I just want to exemplify the point that we can either focus on our
goals or focus on the process. I respect and honour the right of
every person to practise whatever they choose in any way that they
intend. Your intentions will always manifest whatever you do.

Below is the Reiki Second Degree attunement.

REIKI 2nd DEGREE

Only Attunement

STEPS

	1	Stand behind initiate and put your hands on their shoulders	
then			
	2	Sign TAM-A-RA-SHA three times	(六)
then			
	3	Sign CHO-KU-REI once, saying its name three times in your mind	
then			
	4	Sign DAI-KO-MIO once	
then			
	5	Sign CHO-KU-REI once, saying its name three times in your mind	
then			
	6	Sign HON-SHA-ZE-SHO-NEN once	
then			
	7	Sign CHO-KU-REI once, saying its name three times in your mind	
then			
	8	Slide your left hand on back of initiate's neck and place your right hand on the crown to allow energy to flow in	
then			

9   Walk to front of initiate and ask them
    to raise their hand to prayer position

then

10   Sign CHO-KU-REI once each to crown,
     heart and throat; say name in your
     mind three times for each sign

then

11   Take initiate's hands and see these
     symbols in palm of each hand

then

12   Sign CHO-KU-REI once each to crown,
     heart and throat; say name in your
     mind three times for each sign

then

13   Blow puff of breath to crown, heart, throat

then

14   Sign CHO-KU-REI once each to crown,
     heart and throat; say name in your
     mind three times for each sign

then

15   Advise initiate attunement is complete

Congratulations! You are now a qualified Reiki First Degree
and Reiki Second Degree practitioner.

The ability to attune people is the responsibility of the Reiki master. The Reiki master level is the third of seven levels. It is not the top of the ladder or the Seventh Degree. I haven't completed or even attempted the levels of Four through to Seven, so I can't advise you on what's up at those dizzy heights. In some Reiki schools, Level Three is divided into two parts — Reiki 3A and Reiki 3B. Reiki 3A is where the master attunes the initiate into the master energy and Reiki 3B is where the initiate is taught how to teach Reiki and pass on the secret formulae. That is why on all Reiki certification the fully-fledged Reiki master is called a master/teacher or 3A/3B.

The training varies from master to master. Some put their initiates through years of training on the assumption that time makes a more proficient master, while others take shorter times. When I ran 'Healing with Energies' workshops, the process took a weekend. Christine Henderson attuned me into mastery in two hours. In Reiki 3A the initiate receives the full master attunement. However, the initiate is still unaware of the two remaining symbols and the attunement processes. Reiki 3B is where the Master exposes the Reiki Holy Grail to full sunlight. The two symbols taught in Reiki 3B are:

   1. DAI-KO-MIO

   2. TAM-A-RA-SHA

Please note that the Raku and the Tam-A-Ra-Sha are interchangeable symbols in the attunement process. I have seen both used with the same effect.

The master attunement — there is only one — is shown below:

REIKI MASTER

STEPS

1   Stand behind initiate and put your hands on their head

then

2   Sign TAM-A-RA-SHA three times

then

3   Sign CHO-KU-REI once, saying its name three times in your mind

then

4   Sign DAI-KO-MIO once

then

5   Sign CHO-KU-REI once, saying its name three times in your mind

then

6   Sign HON-SHA-ZE-SHO-NEN once

then

7   Sign CHO-KU-REI once, saying its name three times in your mind

then

8   Slide your left hand on back of initiate's neck and place your right hand on the crown to allow energy to flow in

then

9   Walk to front of initiate, gently tap their shoulder and ask them to raise hands to prayer position

then

10   Sign CHO-KU-REI once each to crown, heart and throat; say name in your mind three times for each sign

then

11   Take initiate's hands and see these symbols in palm of each hand

then

12   Sign CHO-KU-REI once each to crown, heart and throat; say name in your mind three times for each sign

then

13   Blow puff of breath to crown, heart, throat

then

14   Sign CHO-KU-REI once each to crown, heart and throat; say name in your mind three times for each sign

then

15   Advise initiate attunement is complete

Congratulations, you are now a fully-fledged Reiki master. By the way, because this is an Eastern-based technology, your lineage is required. Your lineage is the same as a pedigree certificate. To some people the lineage is important because they believe that the closer they are to Usui in descent, the more valuable their status.

When you attune people into mastery, not before, you also give them their lineage. My pedigree looks like this:

Dr. Mikao Usui
Hyashi
Takata
Phyllis Furimoto
Claudia Hoffman
Mary Shaw
Christine Henderson
Bruce Way

As you are attuned by me, albeit distantly, in your lineage your name will go under mine and when you attune people into master status your students' names will go below yours. What about certificates? Just make them up. There is no standard accreditation body, although some associations may tell you differently.

Although I am fully accredited, you may find entry into some Reiki associations difficult. Personally I rejoice at this. Perhaps I am the serpent in the tree suggesting that you are already perfect and that you don't need to join the God Club to prove it. If you want to practise I can assure you that your clients will be drawn to your energy, not your certificate. If they are drawn to your certificate, then watch out. They may want you to live their lives for them.

Now we need to examine the logic of the attunement sequences. You will have noticed that the symbols are the same way in all four Reiki First Degree attunements. You will also notice that the Reiki Second Degree attunement is the same as the first attunement sequence plus the 'imbedding' of the symbols that were taught in the Reiki Second Degree workshop into your hands. The master attunement is the Reiki Second Degree attunement sequence plus the addition of the Dai-Ko-Mio or master symbol into the hands. This is the symbol that enables you to attune others.

In the traditional story of Mikao Usui he discovered the healing sequences but he did not teach Reiki in seven levels. It was

Hyashi, one of his immediate successors, who segmented the approach into levels. Therefore, if we go back to the original story, I suggest that there was only one attunement discovered and that was the attunement to healing mastery. What the neo-Reiki schools have done is to cut this method up into pieces and then teach the pieces. It's sound business sense, I suppose. In the computer industry we call this 'up-selling' or 'value-added selling'. Therefore, blending the components of Reiki First Degree, Reiki Second Degree and Reiki Master graphically look like this:

STEPS

1   Stand behind initiate and put your hands on their shoulders

then

2   Sign TAM-A-RA-SHA three times

then

3   Sign CHO-KU-REI once, saying its name three times in your mind

then

4   Sign DAI-KO-MIO once

then

5   Sign CHO-KU-REI once, saying its name three times in your mind

then

6   Sign HON-SHA-ZE-SHO-NEN once

then

7   Sign CHO-KU-REI once, saying its name three times in your mind

then

8 Slide your left hand on back of initiate's neck and place your right hand on the crown to allow energy to flow in

then

9 Walk to front of initiate and ask them to raise their hand to prayer position

then

10 Sign CHO-KU-REI once each to crown, heart and throat; say name in your mind three times for each sign

then

11 Take initiate's hands and see these symbols in palm of each hand

R1   R2   MASTER

then

12 Proceed as in step 10

then

13 Blow puff of breath to crown, heart, throat

then

14 Proceed as in step 10

then

15 Advise initiate attunement is complete

When I first taught Reiki, I never did one-to-one attunements. I attuned groups of people. That way the size of the group did not hinder the time component of the workshop. I simply guided the audience into a meditation. When they were at rest, I visualised the individuals merging into one amorphous person and then in my mind drew the symbols through all attunement phases. I attuned the audience into Reiki and Seichim mastery at the same time. This also was how I taught. There are several stories that arise out of this approach and the extensions to it.

The first story is set in Queensland, the sunshine state of Australia. Attending the workshop were six Reiki masters who had come out of a genuine interest to hear what I had to say. They were particularly interested in the group attunement method. They chose an excellent workshop for the demonstration, as there were approximately eighty people present. When the workshop finished the masters came to me to attest to the fact that the attunements worked. I flew home and went back to work. A week passed when the telephone rang. 'Hello Bruce, this is George. I am a Reiki master and was at the workshop in Brisbane.'

We chatted for a while and then the question came. He said that a few of them had been trying to copy the group attunement and could not seem to do it. They had concluded that I must have discovered the group attunement symbol. I explained the process that I used, but he insisted that I had the symbol. The more I tried to convince him that I didn't, the more he decided I was hiding it from him.

Then he made me an offer. He said that there were twenty of them prepared to pay me $1000 each plus travel and accommodation expenses if I would teach them how to use the symbol.

Well, $20,000 and a weekend by the beach were very appealing, yet I couldn't do it. After the call, I thought how easy it would be to use people's creative intents and sell it back to them as valuable commodities. In the consulting industry, there is a cynical saying that all a consultant does is to tell the client the time by using the client's watch and then charging them for it. I ask myself if this is what Reiki masters also do. They allow themselves to reflect the person's brilliance back to them.

My early experimental initiates were members of one of my psychic classes. We had sat together for at least two years, so they were used to my antics. These people became the first Reiki and Seichim masters that I attuned. They too are cosmic explorers ready to try anything. Soon after the attunements, Meg telephoned me. 'Bruce, I have been thinking. The actual drawing of each symbol is a process, isn't it?' I answered yes. 'Then can I just visualise the whole symbol for the same effect?' I hadn't thought about it, yet as usual I told her yes. Time passed and Meg rang again. 'Bruce this visualising is working. I am now visualising each attunement sequence as whole instead of signing the sequence, and it works.' I realised that Meg was onto something here. Weeks later, Meg called again. 'Bruce, I hope I haven't done the wrong thing but I am now just visualising the master attunement because that contains the lot. It still is working.'

Meg was actively attuning people. She lived in a country town and many of her friends lived in remote areas. They would ring her and ask for the attunements. She would tell them to hang up the telephone and meditate for twenty minutes and at the same time, Meg attuned them distantly. They were to ring back in twenty minutes and report their experiences. One day Meg rang. 'Bruce, this is getting bizarre. A friend rang for the attunements so I told her what to do. Yet when she hung up another friend knocked on my door. To tell you the truth, I clean forgot about the attunement. When my other friend rang back, she reported exactly the same phenomena as if I had attuned her. Weird.'

Meg was just like the dentist. She was the external symbol for people to express their intentions. When I attune groups I still ask them to meditate. Then I do nothing more than uphold their sincerity, integrity and trust in their infinite spiritual nature. In other words, I revere them as God. Yes, the energy still moves. Reiki masters who have experienced this method declare that they have never felt the power as strong. I rejoice every time I hear that because I know that the energy they are experiencing is the energy of their own wholeness.

You see, the attunement sequences are just a combination of symbols that communicate a specific intention. In the Reiki model, the attunements are saying arise and become a healing master. Initiates do the rest by remembering that they are healers. It is that simple. Therefore, the Reiki master attunement spells out 'healing master'. If we took each letter in the words 'healing master' separately and wrote them on stone, they might just look like symbols. When we put these symbols back together they communicate the intention — healing master. The attunement sequences are nothing special. They are merely invocation rituals asking potential healers to take up their beds and walk.

In the next chapter, I have listed a brief history on Seichim, the symbols and the attunement sequences. The principals of Seichim are the same as those of Reiki. Remember that the Seichim attunements are another language spelling out the same words — 'healing master'.

Oh, incidentally, I want to clarify the following points:

1. No-one to my knowledge has ever been able to verify the traditional story of Dr Usui and his discovery of Reiki energy. Diane Stein in her book *Essential Reiki* notes that research has shown that there are no records that Usui ever attended Doshisha University as either student or teacher. In fact, there is no record of his studying or receiving a degree from the University of Chicago. Diane suggests that the story was Westernised to make the power of Reiki more palatable.

2. Did Usui exist at all? I understand that the portrait photograph on traditional Reiki certificates is not of him.

3. If Usui was real, he never gave certification, so those giving certificates are not teaching his style of Reiki.

4. If Usui was real, he discovered his healing ability by himself. He did not ask another to bestow mastery upon him. He just took it. I suggest that Reiki masters who produce certification are missing part of the message. In any occupation, we are our own certificates! No-one else can bestow our greatness on us.

5. If Usui was real, he never taught the seven levels. Therefore, those teaching the seven levels are also not teaching pure Usui doctrine.

Whether Reiki is real or not has led me to the realisation that as a healing master/practitioner, I am a symbol of a person's external expression of their desire to heal. I can only ask them to take up their bed and walk when I acknowledge that I am whole. The more times that I can acknowledge that I am whole, the closer I will come to the memory that really I am whole. When I know that I am whole then I will no longer have the need to practise as a healer because I will have realised my mastery.

The only question then remaining is: Are we more interested in creating the process than arriving at our destination? Are we more interested in making bread than satisfying our hunger?

Chapter 9

Seichim: Finding Bliss by Playing Jazz Guitar

The philosophy behind Seichim is similar to Reiki. In fact, Seichim is said to be an ancient hands-on healing system discovered by Reiki master Patrick Zeigler.

The word 'Seichim' comes from the Egyptian word 'Sekhem'. It is said to denote the energy emanating from the Goddess Sekmet. This energy was brought to light in a vision that Patrick Zeigler had from a being he believes to have been the Chinese goddess Quanyin. From this encounter another energetic hands-on healing system emerged based on the signing of symbols and attuning people into the energy. When Christine attuned me in the Seichim symbols, there were two levels: the Seichim entry level and the Seichim master level. Since that time Seichim masters have developed several intermediate levels. I cannot help feeling that this is the school teaching bliss realisation through jazz guitar.

Seichim, unlike Reiki, allows for an evolving system within certain guidelines. Reiki rigidly bases its teaching around five symbols whereas Seichim permits the discovery of new symbols and personalised symbols. You will note in the attunement sequences that there is time when the Seichim master allows for new symbols to enter their consciousness. People record these symbols as they come to mind and put them in manuals. I am only going to give you the attunement symbols for entry level and master level. The attunement symbols for Seichim and the attunement sequences are:

Symbols

MAI-YUR-MA

The signing of the MAI-YUR-MA is said to be the gateway to the soul. Practitioners use this symbol to enhance, expand and magnify the physical, emotional and spiritual aspects of love. Notice that the infinity symbol drawn over the heart in the graphic above is drawn three times. This means that the symbol has a power value of three. In Seichim, you can up the power of the symbol to seven or nine simply by drawing the infinity sign seven or nine times.

SEICHIM CHO-KU-REI

In Seichim technology this symbol empowers and magnifies all other symbols. It activates the properties of making things whole. The only difference in this symbol to the Reiki CHO-KU-REI is that the first line is drawn from the right side of the stalk rather than the left side. Drawing the corresponding number of spirals also give this symbol the respective powers of three, seven or nine.

THE LIGHTNING BOLT

The lightning bolt symbol is used for jolting people out of their doldrums and unwanted belief systems.

Here now are the attunement sequences for entry level Seichim and master level Seichim. Each level has one attunement. Notice also the similarity of the attunement sequence for the master level to Reiki Level Two.

SEICHIM ENTRY LEVEL

STEPS

1 Stand behind initiate and put your
hands on their shoulders

then

2 Sign Seichim CHO-KU-REI to value of 9

then

3 Sign CHO-KU-REI once, saying its
name three times in your mind

then

4 Sign TAM-RA-SHA once

then

5 Sign DAI-KO-MIO once

then

6 Sign Seichim CHO-KU-REI once to
value of 9

then

7 Sign Lightning Bolt once and pause; if
any other symbols come to mind, use then

then

8 Sign Seichim CHO-KU-REI once to
value of 9

then

9 Sign HON-SHA-ZE-SHO-NEN once

then

10   Sign Seichim CHO-KU-REI to value of 9

then

11   Place your hands on initiate's head until you
feel the need to finish. If symbols appear, use them

then

12   Put your hands on the back of initiate's neck,
then place your left hand on the back of their
neck and your right hand over their throat;
move your right hand over their heart, move
your right hand over the third eye

then

13   Pause and visualise throat, crown and third eye

then

14   Sign Seichim CHO-KU-REI once to
value of 9

then

15   Move to front and hold initiate's hands and
visualise MAI-YUR-MA to value of 9, and
any other symbols that come to you

then

16   Sign Seichim CHO-KU-REI once to
value of 9, to crown, heart and throat

then

17   Blow to crown, heart and throat

then

18   Advise initiate attunement done

SEICHIM MASTER

STEPS

	1	Stand behind initiate and put your hands on their shoulders
then		
	2	Sign TAM-A-RA-SHA three times
then		
	3	Sign CHO-KU-REI once, saying its name three times in your mind
then		
	4	Sign DAI-KO-MIO once
then		
	5	Sign CHO-KU-REI once
then		
	6	Sign HON-SHA-ZE-SHO-NEN once
then		
	7	Place thumbs on the base of the neck and pump in energy using lightning bolt
then		
	8	Sign CHO-KU-REI once each to crown, once to heart, once to throat
	9	Move to front and take initiate's hand and pump in energy using lightning bolt

then

10   Visualise TAM-A-RA-SHA in both hands

then

11   Sign CHO-KU-REI once each to crown,
heart and throat

then

12   Blow to crown, heart and throat

then

13   Advise attunement done

Chapter 10

The Storyteller 5

Ted was an interesting study. His friends saw him in an inspirational light. 'You always shoot for your dreams,' friends often told him. 'We've rarely met someone with the level of determination that you demonstrate.'

Ted received letters thanking him for his words, his commitment, overall honesty and just plain down-to-earth, no frills, 'this is the way it is' philosophy. People viewed Ted as successful. Yet, all Ted saw was the destruction that followed in the wake of striving for his dreams. In Ted's eyes, he was pig-headed. He thought he was extremely stubborn. He held only one view of the world — his. He obsessively planned his future and pushed most people's lives to one side. Sure, he needed them. They were the marketplace. They were the consumers, whether actual or potential.

Frequently, Ted lost prospective promoters when asked, 'Just who is your audience?'. His reply was always sharp and to the point: 'Everybody'.

'Surely there are segments in the market?' The response was predictable. 'How can we market you when you can't help us to visualise who your market is? Where do we find the "everybodies" in the marketplace? People are so diverse, Ted. You must help us by defining the people that you want to reach.'

Ted would simply respond: 'Everybody is everybody. It's the differences between the "everybodies" that make up the market demand'.

The promoters just couldn't handle this. Marketing 101, 102 and the master's program didn't have a measurement device to identify everybody. Certainly marketing courses needed consistent parameters to slot people into market segments.

'You can't put people into bags,' Ted remonstrated to Abbey.

Abbey had told Ted that she was the marketing genius for him. 'Every person is uniquely brilliant. They just manifest their brilliance in different ways. Just market to everyone,' Ted continued.

'Well, there has to be a common thread. Some unifying strand that binds the marketplace together,' Abbey debated.

Ted thought for a moment. It looked as though Abbey had him stumped. 'Find the need and exploit the deed, hey? Sound marketing I reckon.' Ted's sarcasm cut through the marketer's poise.

'Ted, you have to address this question seriously or we just can't do business together.' Abbey was nearing walk-out point.

'Why can't you just use your intuition to find the answers?' Ted didn't let up. In fact, usually this question opened the exit door for the faint-hearted marketer. Abbey was no exception. She walked like the rest of them.

Ted lived in a fluid state of aloneness. He led a busy life. He had psychic clients queuing for readings. Yet he could no longer find the enthusiasm or drive to help them. He felt guilty that most clients had paid him in advance.

The feeling of aloneness was his constant companion.

Even as Ted tried to develop his speaking business, these words rang true. Promoters volunteered and left. 'We can't work with you. You always have to have it done your way.' Ted established his own business. That way he could be in control. Yet the pattern of never finishing was woven so tightly into the tapestry of Ted's personality that success eluded him.

His motif was: 'Never achieve your brilliance'.

Achieving was an ingrained family trait. Ted came from working-class stock, where tangible achievements were the status symbols of respect. 'It is the things that we do that people will remember us by,' his grandfather told him when he was five. 'And when we've gone to heaven, that's all people will have of us — their memories of what we have achieved.' Just thinking about doing things made him tired. Yes, he could visualise the dreams that excited him and he would make plans. Ted loved to plan. Planning was safe. You can always make the perfect plans, until you tell them to someone else and they try to convince you that your plans just won't work in their world.

This was another aspect of Ted's multitude of foibles. He would become so excited about his dreams that he would tell the world. He would boast about his planned achievements. Ted was a good orator and salesman. The only problem for Ted was that to achieve the dream he had to do something about it.

Ted graduated from high school and gained entry into the prestigious commerce/law degree at Monash University. Someone once asked him why he wanted to go there. 'Because that's where I am going to make a name for myself. That's what I'll do to be remembered.' Strangely, that's what he remembered most about his grandfather. That he had built a successful business from scratch. It's still going today. His brother studied commerce before him and intended to run businesses. So too, his father dreamt of the success from business.

All through first year, Ted strutted. He held his head high and proudly sold his dream. Somewhere in the year he forgot to study, go to lectures or hand in his assignments. Here is the *doing* thing again. Ted failed first year. 'Well, at least I failed to the best of my ability,' he told his cousin. 'Four out of four. Can't fail better than that.' Greg, his cousin, asked him: 'How do you do it? The optimism I mean. I would be devastated'.

Ted butted in. 'There is always tomorrow.' Even in his failure, Ted somehow had the gift of optimism.

Four years passed and Ted optimised his studies by attending three more universities. He shifted to psychology and managed never to complete any courses. He was growing up because Ted now enjoyed the doing. He had mastered Dreaming 101, Planning 102 and Doing 103. He was uncertain about taking the final two courses of the Success degree. They were Implementing Successfully 104 and Completing What You Start 105.

Ted left the university scene. He was clever. He never had openly stated that he quit. He merely convinced the tertiary institutions to throw him out. What a salesman! 'Well, Dad is a salesman and he does all right. I don't need tertiary qualifications for people to respect me. People respect money more and you can make a lot more in business — especially sales.' It seemed like a good story to Ted and he sold it well. So he thought until his newly married wife left him before their first wedding anniversary.

It seemed that Judy couldn't abide the sales speak, the dreams, the flying high. 'Ted, I just can't trust you anymore. Why can't you tell me the truth? Somewhere the sales pitches have transformed into lies.'

'Ah, c'mon! They are not lies. I will just tell you what makes you happy. What's wrong with that?' was Ted's response.

'But nothing you tell me ever happens. You don't do anything to make it happen.'

The door slammed shut. Ted leaned on the outside of the door in the apartment stairwell, bags packed. Judy's definition of leaving was to surgically remove the reason, in this case, Ted, for the cause of the infection that raised her temperature to fever proportions.

'I am telling you, Ted, unless you do something to get your act together, this trial separation will be permanent.'

Ted sighed. 'At least I will have some peace and quiet for a while. No more nagging what I should do. There's still hope. Isn't life great? Another challenge! Another new start! Something to plan for.' He hailed a cab to his new abode.

The separation lasted a year. Ted gave up his job as a commission-only 'wet' T-shirt salesman and joined the Australian Public Service. 'That way I can bludge at work and go back to university and get a degree. That will impress her.' You see, the analogy of excising the wound was apt. Judy was a medical doctor and a smart one at that. Ted settled down to a year of doing. He started at the bottom, as most public servants do, and he rose considerably faster than most.

Ted seemed to have the knack of being in the right place at

the right time. Although he didn't know it, he was uncannily intuitive. Ted chose the federal government department that was growing faster than the unemployment lines in the mid-eighties — the Commonwealth Employment Service. In the eighties unemployment grew in direct relationship to the inflation rate. 'Unemployment is a growth industry,' Ted often joked.

The department had a serious image problem that required marketers. Ted found himself in his element. No one knew about marketing and Ted could bull better than most. He put his hand up for every publicity sales-ish/marketing job that the department advertised. His interviews were filled with comments about market reach, the four 'P's' of marketing, brand identification and so on. Ted discovered that he could weave a credible story around very few known facts.

For the first time in his life, Ted was achieving success. He spoke to businesses, sold candidates and wrote reports. His peers begrudgingly acclaimed him as a rising star. Now he could impress Judy. He was becoming someone. Granted, he wasn't well educated but the money he would make from his newly acquired marketing skills would surely compensate.

On the anniversary of their separation, Judy and Ted reunited — in a conservative way. They began courting again. Judy told Ted that she had to witness his newfound sincerity and commitment to honesty. After all, he had lied to her on repeated occasions so she needed time to trust him again. She also needed to get over the two affairs she had had while they were together in that first year of marriage. She confessed to these to show Ted her commitment to honesty. She felt terrible. 'I had to do it because of your lying. You pushed me into them, I hope you realise.'

In a strange way, Ted actually felt relieved because Judy, by her actions, had endorsed his point of view that lying was okay if the situation was right. Two years later, Ted quietly slipped back through the door of his former marital home permanently. Yes, he had achieved something. He had a good career. 'With good prospects,' he would say. Granted, the public service was not exactly the same as business, but in time …

Time came quicker than Ted thought. Judy and Ted were at a dinner party with a few of her medical colleagues when the axe fell. The conversation centred on the Department of Health's new registration procedures for medical practitioners. 'Bloody public servants!' someone said. 'They are just shiny pants who can't make it in the real world, so they screw us. Hell, we pay their salaries, Goddamn it!'

Ted took another sip from his empty glass. Someone asked him what he did for a crust. 'Oh, ah, I'm in personnel consulting,' he replied.

'Who for?'

'Oh, I can't say. Not allowed. We headhunt in sensitive areas. Better not say,' Ted squirmed.

'Why did you lie about your job?' Judy bailed Ted up in the car on the way home.

'I didn't lie. I just sort of embellished a bit.'

'It's still a lie, no matter what you call it.' Judy was putting on her Mohammed Ali relationship negotiating gloves.

'Judy, I just told a little story. What's wrong with that? No harm done.'

They drove the rest of the way home in silence, parked the car and Judy, still fuming, turned to Ted. 'To tell you the truth, Ted, if I knew you were going to be a public servant before we married, I wouldn't have gone through with it. You, you … conned me, Ted!'

'But Judy, when we married I didn't know that I would join the public service,' Ted whined.

'There you are, then,' she spat back. 'Storytelling is so inbred in you that you don't even know that you are doing it.' With that she flew out of the car, slammed the door and went straight to bed.

A month later, Ted applied for a job at Connect Personnel and got it. 'You are on probation here, Ted,' Warren, the owner and managing director, said. 'Frankly, I think public servants are failures.

You must have told a good story to convince Pauline to hire you. Let's see how you run with it.'

The job at Connect Personnel went extraordinarily well. Ted had the knack to extract from job applicants the truth about their employment histories. He could tell when they were lying or covering up what they considered to be career blotches. Similarly, he knew how to extract an accurate job description from the employer. Ted was a natural for the role. He would listen to both sides, question the gaps and then write the job description and the advertising copy. Usually he would rewrite the job applicant's resume in a more favourable light and fit it to the employer's requirements, which, of course, Ted wrote. Ted's job was all about writing.

The task that Ted enjoyed the most was writing the invoices. After all, the invoice generated his commission, and the more commission he made, the more respectable he became. He could often be heard telling both employer and job seeker alike, 'It's how you tell your story that's going to impress the right candidate/employer'.

Ted's enthusiasm for the role grew, as did his bank account, until the seasons changed. Ted forgot that there was a planning season, an implementation season and a hard work season. He only focused on the 'banking the results' season. Like the English king who believed that he could stop the tides, Ted believed he could stay in the banking season forever. Therefore, he only wrote banking season stories — invoices. However, if there was no reason to write an invoice, nor a client to pay it, the invoice document resembled a fictional account of the dream. The fact that it was dishonest seemed to elude Ted. He just kept writing fiction until Warren fired him.

Ted felt guilty, became repentant but seemed to miss the point of his lies. There was the lie about the false invoices but the greater lie was that Ted presented fiction under the guise of facts. Somewhere in Ted's psyche hid a belief that storytelling was wrong.

Ever optimistic, Ted tried different businesses, eventually

settling into a headhunting business he part-owned. In time, Judy had enough and left Ted. She told him that this time there was no hope at all. There was nothing Ted could do to reconcile the situation. That seemed to suit Ted. The pressure came off and he fell in love again three months later, a fact that didn't slip past Judy.

'You just couldn't wait to find someone else, could you? So much for me waiting around!'

'But Judy, you told me it was over, finished, you know, for good. I believed you.'

Judy scowled. 'Stupid man, don't you know when a person is not telling you everything. God, you are so gullible!'

Elaine was everything that Judy was not. She loved the fact that Ted owned a headhunting company. She celebrated his business successes with him. They were blissfully happy, for a short time at least. A strange thing began happening in Ted's life. His business partner took half their client base and established his own practice. What business was left began to diminish and new business was harder to win.

Ted discovered rebirthing, a regression therapy designed to show a person their true self. He wanted to cut loose from his illusions so that he could find the switch for the light. The more he processed, the worse his business became. Ted's debts grew, yet his skill at convincing his creditors that he was doing well kept them at bay. The business sunk lower and lower. Ted knew he needed to keep Elaine's spirits up so he always spoke optimistically about the future, avoiding the present and reality.

It was after a particularly empowering rebirthing session that Ted found himself sitting at his desk in his office looking out at a bleak, rain-streaked day. The bank had just refused to extend his credit. He had no job briefs. The rain beat in and tried to help by tapping morse code on the window pane. 'Why?' Ted asked himself. 'Why aren't my consultants doing their jobs? I pay them enough.' The rain kept tapping in syncopated rhythm to Ted's heartbeat. 'Why? Why? Bloody, well, why!'

Just at that moment, the window blew open. Rain spattered on the business projections. Ted flew to the window and pulled it shut. 'Can't blame anyone other than myself. Damn, I should have latched the window.' Ted dried the pages as best he could. Even the rain could not smudge the impending tragedy. The rain kept beating. 'Can't blame anyone … should have shut the window … can't blame anyone … should have … The rain eased and transformed to mist. The sun finally squeezed itself through the clouds and the outside world fell silent.

A knock on the door at first jolted him, until he realised that it was Rod, his senior consultant. 'Am I disturbing you?' Rod asked.

Ted looked at Rod, not wanting to hear what he would say. 'Do you want the business?' Ted posed the hypothetical.

'This business? There's not much left of it. I guess I could take it off your hands. Couldn't pay you anything for it, though.' Rod walked to the window and looked out at the steam rising from the pavement.

Ted pulled out a sheet of letterhead. 'Today I pass full title of Explore Australia to Rod Bassinger, understanding that he will not pay me a cent.' Ted signed the note. He took the office keys from his key ring and placed them on the paper. He then slid the lot across the desk towards Rod. 'I guess it's yours then,' Ted said and with that packed his belongings in a box and left.

As Ted walked from the building the sun felt warm on his back. 'Now, that's the craziest thing you've ever done,' he muttered under his breath. 'Why? … Am I going mad?' He walked to the car. 'Can't blame anyone … should have shut the window.' The rhythm continued.

Elaine came home from work to find Ted cooking osso bucco. 'You're home early,' she said, slightly surprised.

'Yeah, I just gave the business to Rod. I realised that I had to move on. Money's going to be tight for a while and I don't have any options,' Ted blurted out, surprised at how quickly the truth came when you took off the optimistic frills.

'How much have we got then?' Elaine tried to stay calm.

'Actually, nothing. I sent the car back this afternoon …' This time the thunder was not sounding from the skies.

'You what? Ted, you mean we have nothing? You told me that everything was fine!' Elaine gasped.

'Everything is fine. We just don't have any money.' Ted offered the olive branch.

'Liar! You liar.' And with that, Elaine spent the night at a girlfriend's place.

Three days later Ted came home to find Elaine and her friends packing her belongings. Then she was gone and Ted was suicidal. Night after night, he lay awake rehashing Elaine's parting words. 'You did this to Judy and you've done this to me. Ted, I want children and you are not going to be their father. I don't want my children having a father who just tells stories all of his life.'

Ted never saw Elaine again and her words rang in his mind intermittently for years to come. 'A father who just tells stories all of his life.' One early morning, as he walked to the kitchen, out of the corner of his eye, he caught a glimpse of a man staring at him from the mirror. The image shook him to his core. He was looking at himself and, for the first time in his life, he hated what he saw.

He ran to the kitchen, put the coffee on and looked in the *Trading Post* to find a rifle. He would kill that man if it were the last thing that he did. Later that morning, the fear was still with him, and the hate was as strong as ever as was the despair. Fear, hate and despair, all good bedfellows except for the despair. You see, the despair was because Ted was so broke that he couldn't even afford to buy a gun to shoot the man in the mirror. He tore up the paper in rage and threw it at the stove — a gas stove. It was equipped with an oven big enough to rest his head in and sleep. 'I can still get the bastard,' Ted muttered, now strategising the gassing.

The wind blew, and the rain came with hail that cracked against the window. 'Can't blame anyone … should have shut the window.' The rat-a-tat started. 'A father who just tells stories all of his life.'

Elaine's voice provided the musical backing to this bizarre solo. 'Can't blame … should have … tells stories … life.' The words became confused and jumbled. Ted could not shut them off. At 3.15 in the morning he reached for the telephone and dialled. 'She's got to be there. Come on. Can't blame anyone … shut the window … tell stories … life.' The telephone rang out. 'Can't blame anyone … should have … told stories … life.' Ted redialled. 'Can't blame anyone … should have … told stories … life.'

'Hello?'

'Ted. Can this wait? We have a session Thursday next.'

'Jacqui, you've got to help me.' Ted paused, searching for the 'it will be all right' words to pad the truth with cushions of optimism.

'What is it, Ted, it's …'

Ted cut in: 'Jacqui, you have to help me. I am so sick. I have never been this ill. I do not want to kill myself but …'

Now it was Jacqui's turn. 'Look, Ted. You woke me up to tell me that. Our appointment is next Thursday. That is three days away. I will see you then.'

'Jacqui, don't hang up. You have to help me. I need healing.'

Jacqui's voice steeled with kindness. 'Ted, I've told you before, I can't help you. If you want to help yourself, then let's talk on Thursday. It's your call.' Click. Jacqui was gone.

Ted dialled again, thinking that there was a line fault.

'Hello. I can't come to the phone right now. I really want to take your call.'

Ted slowly put the handset back on its cradle. The rain kept drizzling down. Ted dressed, put on his coat and walked the streets until sunrise. The further away from the stove the better. Ted knew that he could not trust himself. His life had just compressed into a single focus. He had to get to the meeting with Jacqui on Thursday and find out what she was talking about.

Chapter 11

Walking the Line Between the Opposites

To continue the symbol theme, let's examine the symbol that has virtually become the logo of anything purporting to be natural. It is the symbol representing Taoism.

There are many interpretations of this symbol. Some common ones are that the symbol represents yin and yang, male and female, hot and cold, two polarities of the one, light and dark, balance and duality. The symbol, when viewed from a Western viewpoint, represents the blending of opposites or the duality in life. Note that for this interpretation we need to be able to identify black as black and white as white. We need to identify between male and female, between good and evil, and even between health and illness.

How do we make these distinctions? We distinguish between black and white by associating certain stimuli affecting our vision with certain learned responses. As infants, our parents showed us pictures with colour in them and then taught us the names of the colours. Unless we are colour blind, we have receptors in our eyes that distinguish between certain stimuli. Similarly, we learn to distinguish between males and females. The stimuli might be different yet the socialising or education is the same — find out the specific attributes about an object that is unique to that object, then notice what attributes that object doesn't have. When we can do this, we have developed the ability to be discerning. This helps us progress through our lives by allowing us to establish what is actual and what is not. When preparing this manuscript I was tempted to type the word *real* in place of the word *actual*. However, if we don't make this distinction, it places a very different meaning or slant on our view of the world.

To illustrate this point, I will introduce you to Helen. She is a well-known Australian psychic. The main way that she communicates psychically is via her clairvoyant ability, which is the ability to see things that the general community does not usually consider to be real. To express it another way, clairvoyants see auras, spirit guides, symbols, deceased people and so on. This particular talent is a most sought-after psychic skill. Psychic students often become awe-struck when in the presence of a clairvoyant. 'If only I could do that! Imagine being able to actually see the spirit world!' they often exclaim. In fact, one student said during a lecture that Helen was giving, 'I am so envious'. Helen, on the other hand, seemed unimpressed. Her response was far from supportive.

'Well, at times it has been my greatest curse,' she replied. 'Just imagine having this ability as a child and not being able to distinguish between spirit people and human people,' she continued. Helen then went on to explain that, as a child, she could not discern between physical and non-physical energies. People thought she was strange when she would stop in the street and talk to ... well, they could only see the letterbox. To Helen, spirit people are very real, yet to most of the human population spirit people have no actual relevance to physical reality. Therefore, people who do not recognise spirit beings as real note that Helen is different from them. As we evolve socially, so do our assessments of people and situations. At this stage, note that there is only discernment between different attributes.

The Taoist symbol talks about duality. What happens when we place a value on a discerned attribute? For instance, we associate a moral code with a discerned attribute. It is said that people are social beings. We live in communities, interact with each other, and need each other to breed and so on. As social groups develop, they identify certain behaviours that they consider to be destructive to group cohesion and evolution. When this happens, a social or moral code of behaviour develops and rules form to protect the values of the group. When a person behaves in a way that could be destructive to group goals, people noted for their discerning ability judge the behaviour. The group judges the behaviour either as acceptable or as unacceptable. Now if we introduce a moral code into the equation, humans consider acceptable behaviour as good and unacceptable behaviour as bad. Therefore, the Taoist symbol can also represent good and bad.

When we put healing into the Taoist model we judge a person as either ill or well. In other words, society makes judgments about differences and places them in different camps. Society then defines each camp as opposite to the other. Duality is a characteristic of the karmic model of life, which is linear, in that it states that creation is a result of an action. That is, actions are the causes of results and the results affect us. Can you see how the more we move along the path we build up sequential strings of causal conditioning? Therefore, the karmic or linear world is a world of cause and effect. That is, it is a doing world or a world of action. Experiences then are the result of feeling the effect of actions. In the linear world, we learn via experience.

Yet, ancient Taoists created this symbol to communicate a different message. They said that the path of the righteous person is the path that travels the line between the opposites. Have you ever tried to walk a fine straight line? What happens if, when you start to walk the line, you keep looking to your left at a ninety-degree angle? The chances are that you will move towards the left of the line. The way that you stay on the line is to focus on it as you walk. When we focus on the line, we become unaware of the areas either to the left or to the right of the line. Our activity then focuses on balancing on the line between the opposites. This, then, becomes our world.

The Taoist symbol when viewed from this perspective represents two worlds, each world being opposite to the other. The Taoists also gave us a strategy to move through these two worlds. They said that the way of the righteous is to walk the path between the opposites. Yet, when we look closely at the symbol there appears to be no path. The path does not appear to exist in our world. Is it a real path or is it an actual path? Can we find this path by using our educated and socialised sight? Alternatively, can we find this path by looking through the eyes of the soul? Trying to find the answer to this question can stretch the intellect to the point of creating a migraine. Then hands-on healing becomes useful. Perhaps you have noticed that in my comments I cannot escape the dual notion. The more obvious interpretation of this symbol is one of comparisons of opposite states.

When I explore the Taoist meaning, I find that there is another state created — the state that exists between the opposites. There is also implied in the Taoist comment a comparative or judgmental condition. The Taoists refer to the hidden path between the opposites as the path taken by the righteous. Hold on a minute! Are the Taoists saying that there are two more opposite states in this symbol? If the path between the opposites is the path righteous people walk, then do we assume that another path exists that the unrighteous walk? Here we go back into religion again. Without getting too absorbed into the meanings of words, it appears that the word 'righteous' is associated with the state of being divine. How do we describe God? You have it. We describe God as divine. We also say that God is perfect, immortal, and the creator of everything. We also say that God is timeless. Therefore, God just is. Where does God live? God lives in paradise.

God is all these things AND God is righteous. If the path of the righteous is the line between the opposites AND God walks that path, then the line between the opposites is God's path. This path then is the path of being. Phew! Lucky I figured that one out. Just in time. For a moment, I thought I might try to find this path. If I could walk the path between the opposites then I could ... Gee whiz! The conclusion is unthinkable. They burnt people at the stake for thinking just that. It's … it's … it's heresy! All my life they trained me to believe that I am mortal. I am a sinner and if I do wrong things then I will suffer. I must atone for my mistakes. That's the law of the universe. If I am sick then it is because there is something that I have done that has created my illness. To heal myself I must rid myself of the nasty personality trait, you know, from my lower soul, first. Then I can be pure. Then I can be whole.

If we see only what we believe to be real then I can understand that the person who just experienced a near heart attack in the previous paragraph cannot see the line between the opposites. There appears to be, yet again, two states — righteous and unrighteous. I prefer to take the moral tone from this discussion because, if we allow it to define our frame of reference then science will blind us. I prefer to call the righteous state the state of being and the unrighteous state the state of doing. I need to drag you back into my play *What Turns Me On*. To recap. God lives in a state of being. God has everything including the desire to create. How do you create in a place that has everything? Creating is a doing thing. Yet God lives in a being place. C'mon, let's get reasonable here. How can you do something in a state of being? The two just don't match. So perhaps God has to find a doing state to create in. Perhaps God also knows that to create something forever is to limit you. If you create things forever then when you change your mind, how can you change things? If you create things forever and at some future time want to replace these 'forever' things then you will have to destroy the very things that you created. If you respect all life, then how can you destroy and create at the same time? Do you see how this duality business really gets out of control? Perhaps God created things with use-by dates to solve the problem. Perhaps God calls these creations experiences and codes into the experiences triggers that cancel the creations at pre-arranged times. Perhaps these triggers activate when God has learnt all God can from the experiences God creates.

Perhaps the universe is like a country estate. On the estate is a homestead. The homestead is a place where we can rest up and regenerate after a long day's work. The homestead is a place where we eat, where we rest, where we socialise, where we plan. In other words, the homestead is a place where we can just be. The estate is very large. It has a championship tennis court. When the residents feel the urge to do something, they may very well decide to play a game of tennis. Naturally, they play tennis on a tennis court. On this estate are rainforests, mountain ranges, beaches, everything that a person wants. All they have to do is go to the place where they want to do what the place is set up to do.

Now imagine that you are the owner of this estate. You know who you are. You know your name, your tax file number, your credit card limits. You know all the important things in life. As you are sitting by the fire in the drawing room one evening you ask yourself: 'Is this all there is? I have everything. I can do anything that I want. There always seems to be enough money in my account when I need it. Haven't quite figured out how it gets there. Hey! Who cares anyway? I am so bored. Tomorrow I need to do something.'

You go to the desk drawer and take out a map of your entire estate. Yet at the boundaries there is nothing more. It doesn't show who are your neighbours, where the airport is or how to leave the estate. All it says at your fence line is, 'This is the entire universe'. Depressed, you go to sleep that night and dream you are at the most incredible resort with perfect temperature, all the food you want, great company. It is … well, dare I say it? It is heaven. You swim out to the cocktail bar in the middle of the pool and order a new drink on the cocktail list. It's called A Divine Experience. The bartender, dressed mysteriously in a scaly type of uniform, asks why you want to drink this. You explain to him that it seems like it could be fun. The bartender shakes his head. 'What is it?' you ask.

'The bartender draws closer to you and says, 'I just don't know that you are ready for A Divine Experience'.

You pout. 'Why, I've tried everything else. You will have to do better than that to stop me ordering this drink. What's in it, anyway?'

'Oh, lots of things really.' The bartender looks away to a person diving off the 200-foot waterfall diving board at the end of the pool. 'If you want to have it, who am I to stop you? Just don't blame me if you can't remember a thing.' With that, he pours the drink.

You sign the bill, knowing the bills never seem to get on your account, and sip the drink. It tastes great. Your lips start to go numb. You feel lighter and lighter. Something really exotic is about to happen and you can sense it. 'God, I made the right decision,' you say to yourself. Bliss is rising up from your ... You wake up. You scratch your head as you hear the breeze rustling through the grass. Grass? How did I get here? You stand up and look at the countryside. It's beautiful. It's so peaceful. Something falls from your pocket. It's the map that you were studying last night. It's just as complete as last night. Look, there is the homestead. There is the tennis court. There is the edge of the map that says this is all there is to the universe. There is no more. 'Damn! I wish I knew if that is all that there is,' you think to yourself.

You feel a hint of crispness in the air and note that the light is changing as the sun turns to flaming red and settles for the evening. 'Well, I can't remember getting here,' you think. 'I had better return to the homestead before it gets dark.' You look at the map and in an instant realise that, although every part of your domain is accurately displayed, you don't know where you are in relation to it. There is no big red arrow on the map declaring, 'You are here'. You have all the information that you require but you are lost. You know who you are. You are the owner of the estate but there is no one to tell that to even if someone challenged you to prove it. You have no identification on you. Only you know who you are and, what's more, you no longer are aware that you are dreaming.

I want to make a suggestion here. Catch it if you will.

Somewhere in our eternity we re-met the serpent. The serpent is appealing and usually appears as someone we trust. The serpent genuinely wants to protect us. Sometimes the serpent assumes our identity. He offers to teach us the way the universe works, to give us all the knowledge that we need and more. The serpent keeps on telling us that wisdom is out there in abundance. The serpent sold us a drink at a pool bar. 'Do you want a divine experience?' the serpent asked.

We thought, 'I wonder what a divine experience would be like?', little knowing that we are the divine experience. It's that familiarity thing again. We were so used to being divine that we forgot that we were. By taking the cocktail, we affirmed that we had forgotten who we were and the dream commenced.

I believe that the Taoists were trying to tell us something extra in their symbol. The circle represents the estate. The circle is the whole universe and we reside in the whole universe. Sometimes we become bored living in a state of being so we decided to flex our creative muscles. We therefore leave the homestead and go into the creating fields. These are the fields of duality and impermanence. If we forget who we are while we are away from the homestead, we lose our way and no longer can find our way back to the homestead. The homestead is the place to be. It is the place where we regenerate. The place is so designed that we just can't forget that we are the residents in the divine dwelling.

When we lose our way from the homestead or our creative centre, it is as if we become entrenched in a dream. Illness, I believe, is not the result of doing something bad. It is simply the state when we run out of energy because we have forgotten that we are the source of our energy. Yet, how does one regenerate? By resting, by being still, by being quiet. What happens when we are ill? Usually, we have bed rest or at least we take the opportunity to withdraw from our regular activities, the ones that keep us from remembering who we are. The Nazarene counselled, 'Be still and know that I am God'. Therefore, we can assume that by being still, we can find the road home.

I should really finish the story of the person lost from the homestead in a dream. After years of wandering through the estate, you give up. That is, I am going to stop searching and accept who I am. You sit down under a tree. You don't care any more and you fall asleep. You begin to dream in your dream. In your dream you wake up and look. You are still out in the countryside. There is a person standing next to you. 'Can I help you?' he asks.

'Only if you can tell me how to get home.'

The person looks at you quizzically. 'Why?' he asks. 'You know the way.'

'No, I don't. I have been wandering for years. I thought I could remember but I look out there and get more lost. Please help me.'

The person shakes his head. 'I can't tell you something you know already. But perhaps there is something I can do for you.'

You feel a glimmer of hope. 'Oh, anything you can do I will appreciate.'

The man steps back. 'All I can do is affirm that you are already home.'

'Oh, rubbish! Look out there. Does that look like home to you?'

The man shakes his head, no.

'Do something please,' you beg.

'Maybe I can give you the energy to remember.'

'Oh great!' you think. 'I have told him already that I am lost and all he is going to do is give me the energy to get there. How the hell do I know where 'there' is!'

As if reading your mind the man says, 'There is where your heart is and I can give you energy to take you there'.

'To my heart? What are you, crazy? Why do I want to be where my heart is? Isn't it where I am already?'

'Yes,' the man replies.

'And you are going to take me there?' In disgust, you close your eyes in rage. They cramp shut. 'I can give you the energy to open your eyes,' the man says. 'All I have to do is place my hands on your shoulders. Will you allow me to do that?'

'Well, will it fix me? God! My eyes hurt.'

'All I can do is to give you the energy to assist your quest.'

'So, you are going to give me energy that won't help me and won't show me the way home.'

'It might ease the pain in your eyes.'

With that you gesture impatiently for him to get on with it. The man places his hands on your shoulders. They feel warm and you feel more relaxed. You relax into the energy as you would a warm bath. Time stops. Your worries stop. 'It feels divine,' you say to the man. Silence. No response. Yet the energy is still flowing and you don't want it to stop.

'I so want to go home,' you say to the man. 'It felt so comfortable when I was there. You know, it feels like the energy that you are giving me now. How do you do that?' Silence again. 'Listen, it's okay. I was mad at you before but now I am not. Can we talk? Not a word of reply. 'Are you listening? Are you there?' You open your eyes to confront the man and stand stunned at what you see in front of you. It is your bedroom. It is the very place where your dream started. 'How did I get here?' You turn towards the man. He has gone. All that is in front of you are large French doors that show the whole vista of your estate. On the glass is written: 'You never left. You just forgot to look inward. That's where you stored your memories.'

A kookaburra lands on the patio railing, throws back its head, and laughs and laughs and laughs. Still numb from the effects of your divine cocktail, you sit down. Your eyes fall on a business card on the side table. It reads: 'Ted Ryan — Reiki Master, Seichim Master, Spiritual Healer, Hands-on Healer'. You turn the card over and look at the writing on the back of the card. 'I am looking for my home. If you can help me, my e-mail address is TedRyan@GodOnlyKnows.com'.

Chapter 12

Mandorla Brilliance: Paradox at its Best

A silent thread that ran through the previous chapter was that of the notion of paradox. Whenever we speak about the notion of duality, many contradictions surface to distract us from the line. The Taoists designed their symbol in such a way as to separate the opposites in a situation. Therefore, if we are discussing temperature, for instance, one side of the Taoist symbol will represent heat and the other side will represent cold. So, how do we experience temperatures by walking the line between the opposites? Perhaps the line between the opposites represents a non-temperature zone. We can say, as I imagine the great Taoist poet, Lao Tzu, would, that we experience temperature by not experiencing temperature. In other words, experience is involved in noting the differences or the effects from our behaviour. How do I know that something is hot? I know something is hot by comparing it to a cold state.

I remember an experiment at high school that showed the relativity of perception. We placed a hand in a bowl of hot water. It was very hot. Then we placed the other hand in a bowl of cold water. Yep, it sure was cold. Then we held a block of ice in the hand that formerly occupied the cold water bowl. After a minute or so, we put down the melting ice and placed that hand back into the cold water bowl. Surprisingly, the second time that we placed our hands in the cold water bowl, the cold water felt much warmer. Yet, the temperature of the cold water remained constant.

As an aside, in hands-on healing we observe the energy running through our hands by noting the difference in state as we compare the sensation of experiencing healing energy to what we consider a normal state. As a child I spent a lot of time at the beach. I was always keen to get into the water, even on wintry days. I would dive into the waves and brace myself for the shock of the cold water, yet I knew that if I stayed in the water, my body would soon adjust to the cold and I would feel warm. The water temperature didn't change. I adjusted to my environment. People often call me and say that a Reiki master attuned them and a year or so later the energy doesn't appear as strong. Usually, the concern is that they are somehow losing the energy. All that is really happening is that they are adjusting to the sensation of the energy so that there is no longer a perceptible difference. That is, they have integrated the notion of healing energy into their consciousness. To put this into the Taoist model, on one side there is the sensation of the healing energy and on the other side there is the sensation of the non-healing state. What happens when a person can no longer notice a discernible difference? I suggest that they have come to rest and returned to the line between the opposites.

In this sense, experience is like a swinging pendulum. Imagine the fulcrum of the pendulum to be at the top of the Taoist symbol. The pendulum is centred when it is at rest. While it is centred, I suggest, it is resting on the line between the opposites. We, just as God, enjoy the sensuality of life. We derive, or create, this sensuality through doing things in the linear or karmic world. So, just like God, we decide to leave our homestead and walk through the estate. We say to ourselves, 'Today I want to experience hotness'. We leave our position of non-sensation, the line between the opposites, and we swing out into the hot side of the Taoist symbol. After a while the hotness no longer appeals to us. Perhaps we got sunburnt, a heat rash or just thought that it would be nice to feel the cold and head toward the snow country. We then swing the pendulum back across the line between the opposites and into the cold country.

I suggest that the path that we create, or the arc of the pendulum swing, represents our experiential learning. The pendulum keeps on swinging between the opposites until we learn all we want to about hot or cold and then let the pendulum rest again on the line between the opposites.

Let's put this into a healing setting. A person is at rest on the line when they go for a routine medical check-up. The results of the tests show that this person has high blood pressure, a heart murmur and unless something is done about it quickly, there is a real possibility of a heart attack or a stroke. The doctor urges the patient, and the patient agrees that they should do something. We have previously discussed that intent is the propellant to action. In this case, the intention is to do something about the heart murmur, so instantly the person is in the world of experiences and action.

'What do you suggest?' the patient asks.

'You must change your diet. I will prescribe some drugs to get your blood pressure down and if that doesn't work perhaps it means a surgical bypass operation.'

The patient follows the dietary plan as prescribed, takes the drugs, exercises as directed and three months later there is no change at all. Not wanting an operation, the patient visits a natural therapist, who prescribes herbs for the patient. At the same time, someone suggests that the patient learn to meditate and refers the patient to a hands-on healer.

The experiential movement of the pendulum is now in full swing. Making up the swinging arc are points where the patient experiences different health treatments. All are relevant and viable. They are just different. All of which is experiential learning on various levels. Therefore, while we are experiencing the illness and searching for the cure, we are looking through the French windows of our homestead into the estate where we believe that the cure can be found.

Usually it is after the experiences have finished that understanding takes place. This happens in a state of rest when one can look back on the experiences in a detached frame of mind. This detached space is on the line between the opposites. Similarly, I believe that hands-on healing works because it puts the recipient into a blissful state. Then, for a moment, they enter the domain of wholeness and have the opportunity to remember that they never left the homestead.

The Buddhists call the state of detachment being equanimous. A style of meditation, called Vipassanna, exemplifies this point. Proponents of Vipassanna meditation maintain that when we take the focus off a physical disease and drop all judgment about it, then healing takes place. They teach Vipassanna meditation as a way of disciplining ourselves to be equanimous. This meditative technique is a process of mentally scanning the body, noting where there is a sensation and then moving on from it without focusing or even trying to identify the sensation. The ultimate test of Vipassanna meditators is to sit still without any movement for long periods of time.

Many years ago, I decided to try this technique. I enrolled in a ten-day Vipassanna retreat. Every session the teacher would sit on a raised platform in full lotus position. He taught by demonstrating the technique. The teacher would sit, sometimes for three hours at a stretch, without moving a muscle. Now, I was not even close to that. I think I could sit for about a minute.

The problem was that at some time during the ten days, I, as with all participants, would receive an invitation to sit in a small group on the stage with the teacher and practise Vipassanna meditation. I vividly remember the moment — after six days of trying — when a helper gently tapped me on the shoulder and indicated that it was my turn. As I was walking up to the stage with a group of five, I looked at my watch. 'Bruce,' I said to myself, 'just take the pain for five minutes. That's all you have to do. Whatever happens just take the pain and sit still for five minutes. That is your goal.'

We were shown where to sit and as I was shuffling into a crossed-legged position of sorts I looked at my watch. 'C'mon you can do it for just five minutes.' I closed my eyes and the next thing I remember the helper was tapping me on my shoulder and ushering me back to my seat. I glanced at my watch. I had sat still without moving a muscle for thirty minutes! At that moment I knew how the teacher taught. The teacher was a person who could take our pain and process it for us. By doing this, he could give us a Vipassanna meditative experience so we would know what to aim for. At the end of the thirty minutes, there was the tap on the shoulder and we returned to our seats to practise for ourselves.

I think hands-on healing is similar. When a client comes for a healing, they are saying to the hands-on practitioner: 'It is my intention to remember that I am whole. Will you show me the memory, please?'. The hands-on practitioner delivers the energy and puts the client on the line between the opposites, for the duration of the session. At the end of the session the practitioner taps the client on the shoulder and says, as the Vipassanna teacher did, now go and find that state for yourself.

In the healing sense, the Taoist symbol represents many opposites. The most obvious is that health occupies one side of the symbol and illness occupies the other. The symbol also represents wholeness. This begs the question: How can a person be ill and well at the same time? Moreover, with this question we dive into the world of paradox. Simply put, a paradox exists when there are two events that we believe can't exist at the same time.

For example, if I own a house and I find a new house I want to buy, I might say that I can't buy the new house until I sell the old one. That's the paradox. Two states of consciousness that do not appear to be able to exist together at the same time. Robert Johnston in his book *Owning Your Own Shadow* says that there is always a place where the opposing or paradoxical views overlap.

He calls the oval shape of the overlap the Mandorla. Johnston maintains that the Mandorla is the place where God creates. It is the place that contains all possibilities. He says that when we are confronted with a problem, usually it presents itself in paradoxical form. That is, I can have one or the other but not both. Johnston asserts the divine mind knows it can have both at the same time.

Limited thinking represents the problem this way: either I'll live in Sydney or I'll live in the bush. Johnston maintains that some place will exist that will combine the benefits from bush living and the benefits from Sydney life. Restrictive thought assumes a linear stance and works with words such as 'either' and 'or', whereas enlightened Mandorla thinking uses the word 'and' to bind the two opposing states together.

Johnston asserts that the door resides in the Mandorla. If you want to live in the bush and the city at the same time, then the solution will arise when you accept that you can have both situations simultaneously. When you work on Mandorla strategy, the solution will present itself, in a way that you may not have considered.

I might say to a friend, 'I've found the house that I want to buy but I can't buy it unless I can sell my existing house'. Words such as, 'I have to' or 'I want this but' or 'if only' are the hints to tell us that we are trying to create from our finite personalities. The 'if only' syndrome is a sign of illness. That is, the person who remarks 'If only I could do this, then I can achieve that' is actually saying that they have forgotten the memory that they are whole. They have forgotten where the God part of them lives. Remember the statement in Chapter 4. 'I am well and so is the cancer'. This is a magnificent example of placing oneself in the Mandorla. The usual comment would be, 'If only I could rid myself of the cancer then I could be healthy'. Sitting in the Mandorla is walking along the line between the opposites. Using the 'if only' approach means positioning ourselves on the pendulum swing of experience. There we swing from one state to another. At some time, the pendulum will run out of energy and come back to rest. When it does, it comes to rest on the line between the opposites or in the Mandorla. Whichever way you choose to view it, when it comes to rest, we have another chance to remember that we are back at the homestead.

Chapter 13

The Storyteller 6

'We should be refuelling at Bangkok in about an hour.' Bob looked at his watch. 'Have we been in the air that long?'

Ted stretched. His mouth felt as if slow-acting glue held it in place. He must have slept because he could remember very little since the dinner break. Sleep, the gateway into the subconscious and worlds beyond. The only problem, as far as Ted was concerned, was that he had to return to the harsh reality of his present situation. When the flight touched down at Bangkok International Airport, the journey was half over. Ted's mind drifted back to Psychology 101. He always remembered the three different conflict situations. 'Which one am I in now?' he thought. Approach-avoidance, that's it. On the one hand, arriving at Bangkok meant that he could walk around the airport for an hour, stretch his legs, duck into the Qantas lounge and freshen up. That's the approach part. The enjoyable part. The avoidance part was the knowledge that he was halfway home. The time was shortening until he had to face the realities waiting for him.

There was no way to make, or even pretend, the situation was palatable. Ted reflected that he could easily have slipped into stories of optimism. Yet, he knew now with a pragmatism born from hard work and a lot of processing that he couldn't live in the fantasy forever. Nor, in reality did he want to. Life was full of passionate searching for truths. He had connected with his soul. He knew how his soul wanted to express into the physical world. He knew just what watermark that his soul wanted to leave. He was passionate about that. Although he had entirely underestimated the time and effort it took. Every day presented challenges that he needed to transcend. Yet, hidden in the challenges of the moment was the infinite unborn potential of future expression.

The journey to date, although painful, had been worth it. He knew where his future lay, yet it seemed more illusive than the illusions he used to spin in times past. Now nine hours from home he still could not strategise his future. 'Failing for the sake of learning and growth sure sucks,' he commented to himself.

Bob must have heard Ted's mind crying out. 'Well, how's the search for the golden threads going?'

'Does this man ever give up?' Ted squirmed in his business class seat. He knew that Bob would not give up. 'I give up,' Ted responded. He thought if he feigned checkmate Bob might fall for the move.

'That's great. Most positive,' Bob declared with a newfound fervour that took Ted absolutely by surprise.

'Good?' Ted stuttered. 'How can giving up be good?'

Bob put his book away, signalling the chess game was back in full swing. 'When we give up, our minds go silent. We don't care any more. So there is nothing to stop the memory of who we are from manifesting in our consciousness. I often think that is the beauty of illness. It gives us time to reflect and think. When we wear our minds out, we rest. And bingo! All sorts of memories appear. I bet that's how your hands-on healing works.'

Now Ted was taken aback. Who was Bob anyway? How did he know so much?

'Think about it,' Bob continued. 'When you put your hands on someone it relaxes them. They feel safe and quite often go into a light trance. That's when it can happen.'

'What can happen, Bob?'

'That's when the memory of the thread theory can emerge again. Haven't you ever wondered why people who report a near-death experience say that their lives flash before their eyes?'

Ted admitted that he had wondered just that.

'Well, it is just a way for the soul to show them the threads. In my opinion that's why some people totally refocus after the experience. They seem calmer and more positive about achieving their goals. Usually they go about life in a totally different manner than before the experience.'

'You seem to know something about healing.' Now it was Ted's turn to probe.

Bob looked down at his feet. 'I know something about death. My wife died three years ago. I thought that it was so unfair at the time. When you get to my age death is all around you. Whenever I travel extensively, I wonder which friends will be at the dinner parties when I return. I imagine my friends wonder whether I will return at all.'

Ted was about to interject, when a wave of energy swept over him that blanked his mind for an instant. Just enough time for Bob to continue.

'When Martha died I closed the house, packed my bags and purchased an around-the-world ticket. I just could not face sitting in that place alone. The next year felt as if I had sat on aeroplanes for most of the time. I visited friends all over the world, followed my children and went to the occasional seminar. I realised that I had lived my life for Martha and the children. I don't regret any of it. Yet with Martha gone I began to wonder what my life had been all about. What I wanted written on my tombstone. Had I done all the things that I wanted to?

I attended a conference somewhere in North America and a fellow spoke about achieving your potential. I didn't know if I had, so I booked into the session. What he said changed my life. I realised that I had, albeit unknowingly, time and time again in my life expressed my life's purpose. I bought his books and listened to his tapes. He was inspirational. He gently encouraged us to find the courage to look into the shadows of our lives and face our fears.'

Ted interrupted. 'I guess we all have parts of our past that we would prefer to forget.'

'Ah yes,' Bob responded. 'But there is more to the shadowy side of our natures than just using them as a garbage dump for unpleasant experiences.'

Ted grimaced.

'I will explain,' Bob continued. 'Have you heard the saying that goes something like, "Our deepest fear is not that we are inadequate …"'

Ted butted in enthusiastically. '"Our deepest fear is that we are powerful beyond measure. It's not our light but our darkness that most frightens us."' Yes, it's an ancient Sufi saying. I use it all the time in my workshops.'

'I have memorised these words and now hold them dear to my heart.' Bob's eyes shone as he recited: '"We were born to make manifest the glory of God that is within us. It's not just in some of us, it's in everyone"'. Bob looked at Ted. 'You see, it's our shadow side that holds our brilliance. It's in the shadow side that we have the encoding of our lives as gods. Humans have got it all around the wrong way.' Ted began to speak but Bob was on a roll and wouldn't be stopped. 'The saying continues, "… as we are liberated from our own fear …". You see, it's the fear that stops us from looking into our shadow side. After listening to the man in America, I realised that the shadow side of our personalities holds all those things that we can't accept or face as real. Therefore, we hide our hurtful experiences in an attempt to convince ourselves that they are not real. This is the classic stance of Jungian psychologists. Yet, the shadow contains more than unpleasant memories. It holds all those things that we can't accept about ourselves including the dreams that we had as children of magnificent feats. The shadow side of us holds our brilliance potential. It holds the memory that we are who, I mean, that we are God. Therefore, if you have an ambition that you have difficulty realising then the chances are that it is your fear that is stopping you from getting into the shadow to view yourself in all your glory.'

Ted sensed the energy coming from Bob. It felt like the energy in his healing sessions. However, Bob wasn't a healer, he was a retired businessman. 'How do you look into your shadow side, then?' Ted's question was far more than academic. 'Look, I have a point to the question. I have always wanted to write. Every time I begin, the whole world blows up in my face. I run out of money. The family complains that I am selfish and the distractions, I tell you, the distractions come from everywhere.'

Bob smiled. 'That's why you need to find the thread. Just the end of the thread is enough because when you follow the thread it will lead you into the shadow side. I must caution you, though. You will remain safe in the shadow side while you are holding on to the thread. If the unpleasant experiences distract you, it is more likely than not that you will forget to hold on, let go and become detached from the purpose of your life. It's my experience that it is the time that people let go of their special threads that illness begins. Sure, the symptoms may not manifest for years yet they will in time turn up. Hands-on healing, I discovered, takes the panic out of being lost in the darkness. It calms you so that you can begin the search for the thread. Hands-on healing simply provides the most suitable environment for the person to search for the thread. So often the healing induces stillness within the person that is most profound and in the stillness they can see God. The Bible asks us to listen for the still, small voice of God. Well, I think that you can hear the voice in the shadow side. I also think that the voice of God attaches to each person's unique thread. When people follow their threads then they find the pot of gold at the end of the rainbow. That is, they find their absolute creative potential, something that their consciousness has difficulty accepting. That's why they journey into the shadow to find it.'

Bob was alive and his energy lit Ted up with enthusiasm. 'I define creativity as another expression for God.'

Bob looked at Ted and sighed. 'There you are, then. God is your creative expression. You are your creative expression, therefore …'

'I am God,' Ted finished the sentence.

'That's the positive nature of illness, I believe,' Bob continued. 'It signals to people that it is time to face their fears, be still, find the thread and journey into their shadow nature. Illness is the most empowering condition that I know of. Illness signals that it is time for people to face their fears, transcend them and discover who they are.'

'It's easy to say all this, Bob. I know what my purpose is and it still isn't working.' Ted never could stay on the high for long. He always had to introduce a touch of drama.

'Ted, you should have been at the lecture. The man who delivered it was so present. I asked the same question and he replied by quoting Goethe:

Until one is committed there is always hesitancy, a chance to draw back, always ineffectiveness. Concerning all acts of initiative (and creation) there is one elementary truth, the ignorance of which kills countless ideas and splendid plans. That the moment one definitely commits oneself, then providence moves too. All sorts of things occur to help one that would never have occurred. A whole stream of events issues from the decision, raising one's favour in all manner of unseen incidents and meetings and material assistance which no man could have dreamt would come his way.

Bob looked Ted straight in the eye. 'I looked back over my life and could see it. All those things that I was committed to, I achieved. Those things that I was not committed to only presented problems that hindered my commitment. I also realised that the problems I created were also positives because they were the signposts directing me to my fears. Hence the shadow side. I found that I could only overcome my fears by being committed to my dreams. When you venture into the shadowy domains then you must be committed to look for the light not the darkness. Ted, let's leave it here. All I want to say to you is that you are succeeding. From everything that you have said, it's obvious. Yet, the results are not what you want because you are not committed to them. Find the thread. Journey into the shadow and find your Holy Grail. God! I wish you could have heard what the man said in America.'

Ted looked out the window. It was daylight and they were landing in Bangkok.

'I am breaking my journey here,' Bob told Ted. 'I had the whim while you were sleeping to spend some time in Tuscany. I'll change my flight and head for Rome.' Bob pulled out a package and handed it to Ted. 'Also while you were asleep I decided to give you that speaker's book. There's a inscription in it to me. It helped me through the pain of Martha's death. Perhaps you can use it in your talks. Ted, it has been a real pleasure.'

With that, he unclipped his seatbelt, packed his belongings and disappeared out the exit. Bangkok Airport swallowed him instantly. Ted looked at the package. There was a note on the outside. It read: 'You have ten hours of peace. The perfect time to find the thread. Promise me that you will not unwrap this gift until you have found the thread and are committed to it.'

Chapter 14

The Storyteller 7

The hour went quickly, too quickly for Ted. Everything that Bob had said made sense to him. He envied Bob for being able to sit at the feet of a master speaker. 'They always get the best in the States,' Bob had said. His reality was that he was still scared. Real life seemed far from his dreams. As he filed through the check-in gate, he made a mental note to enjoy the rest of the flight. It might just be his last for a very long time. Qantas had reallocated Bob's seat next to a Cardinal of the Catholic persuasion. The man seemed important. Too important to notice him, Ted hoped. Most of the flight would be in darkness so here was his opportunity to sleep, dream and perhaps a miracle would happen and he would find the thread.

'Hello, I am Cardinal Quincy,' the cleric said as he stripped the white collar off. 'I met a friend of yours, Bob, on the way in. Knew him years ago when he was in my diocese. He is a kind man. It doesn't pay to cross him, though. I joked with him that he still could use the confessional.'

'How did you meet?' Ted queried, suspicious.

'Bob was doing some duty-free shopping before he re-routed. Coincidences never cease to amaze me. I am just returning from meetings in Rome and Bob decided to go there. I had been holding a letter from Martha for him for years and now ... God moves in mysterious ways.'

Ted grunted, not wanting to get into a conversation about God with this man. Their views would be poles apart.

'Bob asked me to leave you alone on the trip. He said that you were travelling along the thread towards God. He thought that you needed all the time that you could get. If I can help in any way, I am right next to you. Barry's my name.'

Ted nodded and looked at the in-flight menu. That worked with Bob. Then he realised that he didn't need to worry. The Cardinal had snuggled into his pillow and was preparing to sleep. Ted looked around the cabin. He took out a pad and wrote a poem. The passion to write was always with him.

He remembered when the desire arose from … somewhere, perhaps from his shadow. He remembered his first book. The passion that he had to put it on bookshelves. The fact that he had to initially self-publish. He remembered when a publisher picked it up. The excitement of the publicity tour. He remembered being asked by the publisher what he had in the pipeline and he had nothing much. Now one thing that had come out of the tour was that he had time to put together his thoughts into a portfolio of ideas. From no ideas six years before, he had to stop at twenty. He had ideas for books, plays, movies and poetry. Now his dilemma was to know where to start. Something had happened in the six years since his fortieth birthday. Yes, now he knew what he wanted to do. He just didn't know how to fit it into his daily responsibilities.

He had faced his fears in the early days — fear of failure, fear of speaking, and fear of acceptance. Now his fears were more pragmatic. Fears about paying the rent on time and satisfying his creditors, giving his family what they required. Although he had not written a lot in the past two years, he noted how his writing style had shifted. He thought it had matured. His creativity was flourishing but his business ability, of which financials were a part, was not healthy. Reality was that financially he was sick. Without the financial backing, he could do nothing except sit in the silence of a plane flying across the Pacific Ocean. He could not plan because he had nothing to plan with. He could not visualise because he had smashed all his business opportunities before departure three months prior. He was flying into the void. Every time his mind raced, trying to find a business deal, who he could approach to manage a company, who needed a sales manager and so on, his mind just locked up.

Ted leaned back into the seat, adjusted the headrest and prepared for sleep. 'Until one is committed … until one is committed … until one is committed.' The words were his lullaby for this venture into the blackness. Somewhere out of his memory banks rose the memories of the motion picture *Field of Dreams*. He loved that movie. 'Until one is committed … build the field and they will come … until one is committed … build the field and they will come.' Ted slept until the plane hit rough weather that jolted him back into the moment. He looked at the Cardinal, who awoke at the same time. The Cardinal looked at him with the same steely blue eyes as Bob and spoke directly to Ted.

'Build the field and they will come. Understand this and apply it. You don't play baseball on their behalf. You build the opportunity for them to satisfy their life's purpose, life's passion. Professional baseball players won't play on a substandard field. They will, however, advise you how to build it so that they can play. You are the light. You are the player who will attract the crowds and the spectators. At present, you are playing to the professional players. You are playing to those who are committed to their journey. Your role is to inspire them to keep playing. Your audiences are the spectators. They are those who come to feel a moment of pleasure and to dream. This is the evolutionary process. And when they are ready — whenever that is — then they will decide to stand on the field and become involved. You can't force them. You just keep on playing for them until one by one they think, "I can do this". Then their journeys start towards their spiritual paths. Not before. Your role is to inspire them to create in the physical realms. It is in the physical that the gods play. Why? Because the gods are still trying to understand who they are! You teach the Mandorla, yet you see the two realms — spiritual and physical — as separate. Find the Mandorla to this paradox, Ted. Then you will have found the Holy Grail. Just imagine the physical and spiritual existing together as one. This is the New Jerusalem. This is heaven and earth. Not heaven on earth, as the theologians talk about it. To go to heaven means we leave earth. To bring heaven on earth still assumes separateness. Heaven and earth are existing as one. Find the Mandorla and live in it. When sitting in the Mandorla you will see no difference, you will see no division. Find the Mandorla and build it, create it. The Mandorla is the playing field that people from the spiritual and material will come to sit around and watch the performance. Then they will return to their states and talk about it as if they were a part of it. *People go to experience things that they don't believe that they have.* That is the hook. That is the bait, the enticement. Understand this and you will fill any stadium in the world.'

Ted stared at the Cardinal. 'Why did you tell me this?' he queried.

'I thought you wanted the definition of a master. That's what you teach, don't you — mastery of the self?' The Cardinal smiled. 'Ted, the arena for you is not baseball. You must find the arena. When you have, then commit yourself to playing on it, whether there be none or a million spectators.'

Ted stared at the Cardinal.

'Ted, you have all the signs. You teach healing yet you have failed to identify your illness. The symptoms manifest in the material world. They don't start there. Think about it. You are killing your soul. Now is the time to heal yourself. For Christ's sake, take up your bed and walk!'

The sunrise is always spectacular from 30,000 feet. Light streamed in through the porthole, swallowing the Cardinal in light. Ted tried to look through the light but couldn't. The Cardinal had gone.

'Excuse me sir?' The stewardess politely tapped Ted on the shoulder. 'It's time to wake up. We will be landing in two hours and breakfast will be served soon.'

Ted rubbed his eyes. It was still dark although there was a reddish tinge hinting at the sunrise.

'Can you wake the Cardinal?' she asked

Ted looked at the Cardinal's sleeping form. He touched him

gently on the shoulder. The Cardinal stirred. 'That was some speech you gave to me,' Ted said.

'Speech?' The Cardinal looked confused. 'What speech? I have slept for most of the journey. Kept dreaming about Bob.'

Ted looked across the aisle to avoid the Cardinal's gaze. 'I am a storyteller,' he said to himself. 'And that's what I commit to now.' Ted was no longer religious, yet said a silent something to the universe. 'Business is my illness. It's not the enabler of my writing. I don't need to be like my dad, my brother or anyone. I need to be like me. Writing is my business. Pretending to be the businessman is the lie. That's the illusion, that's the cancer. When I get back home, that is what I will commit myself to, no matter what. I must restore the balance. I must transcend my fears.'

Ted looked into the pocket in front of him. Bob's brown paper package had perched itself precariously on the flap. Thanks, Bob. He reached for the parcel and opened it. To his amazement, it was a well-marked copy of his first book. Ted opened the flyleaf and saw his handwriting. It said, 'To Bob, Mexico, 1996' and then the inscription:

> In the darkness of despair, we find the light that heals,
> Along the path of illness, we find our divinity,
> In our divinity, we find our mastery.
> So to those who choose illness,
> May you find the Grail that you so passionately seek,
> May your courage inspire humanity's transcendence,
> And may you dance through the universe,
> Truly gods of your domain.

Bob had added these words: 'Ted, I enjoyed our conversation. You are as inspiring now as you were in '96. All I gave you were the words you gave to me. A rule of the universe is that we teach what we need to learn. That's the path of the masters. Take up your bed and walk. You can heal yourself — no one else can'.

Chapter 15

Illness: A Path to Transcendence

I want to delve into some homespun philosophy of life. In *Healing Energies* I have tried to express the concept of healing as a process or a journey towards discovering who we are. These ideas may seem radical to you or may touch a chord somewhere within you. I stress that these thoughts have evolved from my observations and you should view them in the light of my personal experiential learning. Who really knows if what I have said is only a rationalisation of a state we call illness in order to ease the discomfort that it causes me to see people suffer. Perhaps none of what I have said has an ounce of truth to it. Yet, it is what I believe.

In the last session of the 'Healing with Energies' workshops, I sometimes conclude with the underlying philosophy that motivates me to be involved in the healing fraternities. Sometimes I have excluded this section from the course. Frankly, this chapter has little bearing on a person's healing journey — unless they catch a glimpse of what I believe.

My background is one of moving from a conservative Christian upbringing to a not-so-conservative individual philosophy. This is my pendulum swing in relation to an understanding of the meaning of life. It is my quest for the Holy Grail. As I developed as a psychic, I was fortunate to find teachers who were well versed in the spirit worlds. Most of them had been involved and some still are with the spiritualist church movement. Although I am not a spiritualist, I respect their teachings, sincerity and dedication. On many occasions I have heard my teachers and mentors from this period say, as indeed do many a spirit guide at a trance session, that there is a long queue of beings just waiting to get into our world. On more than one occasion I have thought, if only I could get out to the queue and tell them that our life may not be all that it has been advertised to be!

Furthermore, my mentors would say that our physical deaths were a sign that we had completed or graduated from this particular life. A nice thought that never rang true to me. So I began to think, why is there this purported long line of spirit beings waiting to get through the turnstiles of earthly performance? My mentors also said that once we physically died we returned to the spirit realms, and viewed and assessed our performance in the physical world and integrated the learning from those experiences. The question in my mind was: What is it that spirit beings want to learn to come into the physical?

Physical World   *Spirit World*

If thoughts create our reality, then what we think is true actually comes true. I began to question what is the difference between the spirit and physical worlds. The only difference that I could come up with was that in the physical world, people commonly accept that our soul and spirit are immortal and that the physical body is mortal. That is, it dies. In the spirit world, the difference is that there is no physical body — well, a body as we know it. Although I have moved on from my Christian upbringing, I am still intrigued at the example of the man whom the entire Christian movement holds as its icon — that is, Jesus the Nazarene.

Here was a master who indeed set the world on its ear. He walked the earth. He turned water into wine. He healed the sick. He walked on water. In fact, he seemed to do all the things that our consciousness thought to be impossible. As his grand finale, he allowed himself to be killed and came to life again. Even if the sceptics amongst us want to dispute the claims of Christians about the feats of the Nazarene, even if we take the story as a myth, it still contains the same message.

When Jesus walked from the tomb, he was intact. That is, his physical body was living as well as his soul and spirit. Most Christians stop the tape there. The story of the Nazarene does not finish with his resurrection. Some time after he raised himself from the dead and having seen enough people to convince them that he was not a ghost he 'ascended to heaven'. Note that he ascended with his physical body intact. Therefore, he did not have to die to change states. There are other biblical examples of this type of transcendence happening. Other cultures also have similar occurrences. Yogis announce the time of their departure from this world, then sit and just leave their bodies. Other gurus on leaving the physical predict the where, when and what of their next incarnation.

The reason to incarnate into the physical world is to learn through experiential expression. Perhaps we come into this dimension to realise that we are whole and that there are no limits. That way there is no karma or judgmental cause and effect. Perhaps we incarnate into this dimension to overcome the notion that we physically die. That is, we come in to transcend our consciousness of limited belief systems. Perhaps illness is the tool that we create to lead us to the memories that tell us that we are whole. Perhaps all that we face in our lives that leads to death are just opportunities for us to flex our divine muscles. Perhaps every challenge is another opportunity to convince us that we are perfect. Every time that we think that ill health or any obstacle is insurmountable, perhaps we have just taken the divine experience cocktail that numbs our perception that we are divine. Perhaps we create paradoxes to learn not to view them as impossible. Perhaps ....

It seems to me that every event in life that creates fear in us gives us the opportunity to transcend our fears and limitations. Every disease presents us with the opportunity to heal. Perhaps the whole of existence is a conspiracy aimed at seducing us into the Mandorla. Perhaps finding health is a game that encourages us to walk the line between the opposites. Perhaps if we play the game of life and death often, we will realise that we can return at will to the source of life. Perhaps at the time of physical death people actually have the opportunity to remember that they are whole and to transcend the consciousness of death. Perhaps, just like the Nazarene, a person recreates a new body as they move into the state of perfection. Perhaps all life is another experiential journey where we can remember who we are and that we are whole, and therefore take up our bed and walk.

Chapter 16

(Epilogue)
The Storyteller 8

QF 2 Heathrow to Sydney via Bangkok touched down on cue. For Ted, the party and adventure of the past thirteen weeks was over. He looked out at the planes waiting in the launch queue to carry their passengers to far-off destinations. New starts for some. New horizons. New challenges. Then there were those going home. Some relieved. Some remorseful. Some just plain tired. He mused that every seat on every plane held a different set of possibilities, a different set of ambitions. Each seat symbolised a resting place for journeying creators. All of them different, yet all living life passionately according to a divine personalised plan hidden from view. These divine plans were tucked away in obscure corners of the psyche waiting for discovery.

For Ted, his was a journey to teach healing. You make masters of those who have the courage to suggest that they have infinite potential to create. When Ted departed thirteen weeks prior, little did he realise that those people waiting for him on distant shores were his masters preparing to acknowledge his intent to heal. 'The exchange is always perfect,' he thought. 'I acted as the symbol of their intentions when I attuned them into mastery. They, in turn, initiated me by allowing me to practise as a healing master.'

Ted recovered his bags from the carousel. He bent down and ripped off the orange priority stickers. 'No one is more important than another no matter how much money they pay,' he mused. 'Reality is that we are our own priority stickers. We are our own certificates of accomplishment. It is our responsibility to see ourselves as priorities. Otherwise we may wander from our soul's desires to create.' Ted was lost when he flew out thirteen weeks prior. He didn't know it. That's the irony. He found himself by realising he was lost. That's the paradox.

'Been away from home long?' the immigration official quizzed. Ted looked at him and smiled. 'Home is where the heart is.'

The official looked through his passport and without looking up, he asked, 'Well where is your heart?' and handed the documents back to him. Ted stood transfixed trying to answer. 'Next.' The official beckoned Ted to move on.

'Where is my heart?' Ted asked himself as he pushed the luggage trolley towards the exit. 'Where is my heart? I know where it is not. To hell with trying to be the great businessman. The only time I think I find my heart is when I create something. When do I feel at home creating? When I am telling stories. So perhaps storytelling is a tool I can use to find where my heart is. When I write I go into the silence. It's in the silence that my heart lives. That is what healing does too. It puts clients into the silence so they can find their hearts. Then their hearts will tell them what tools they can use to find themselves.'

Clarity dawned as had the sunrise earlier. 'Illness then is the soul's way of asking us to find our hearts when we have strayed too far from the homestead. Problems in our lives are simply disguised opportunities to prove again and again and again that we can transcend our beliefs. Losses represent that we have outlived the usefulness of the object we have lost.' Ted looked up. He was back in the airport walking through the reuniting corridor of people. He saw Marianne standing five yards in front of him. There were tears in her eyes. She was smiling. Ted smiled back. He knew at least one place where his heart lived. They embraced.

'Well, how is the healing master?' she quipped.

'The healing master?' Ted thought for a second. 'He has just got off his bed and is walking.'

Ted told Marianne that day that he would never re-enter business as a manager for anyone else. 'I am a storyteller,' he told her. 'The universe will honour that when I do.'

'What about the creditors, how will you pay them?' Marianne asked.

'My parents were wrong.' he replied.

Marianne frowned.

He said: 'I am sure there is money in storytelling. I know that and that is all that matters. Most of my creditors invested in my talent. My talent will pay them back'.

Two months later the courts declared Ted bankrupt. A friend who lent him money to advance his writing was tired of Ted's procrastination over the years. She said, 'Ted, I have got to stop you doing this to others'.

Ted took this to mean selling his dream yet not doing anything about it.

'It's a shame you went bankrupt. Geraldine really went back on her word. Why didn't you fight it?' Ted's friends said.

Ted's response was: 'It's the best thing that has happened to me in years. For the next three years, the Australian government has taken away the temptation to go back into business. Now I have to repay everyone from my talent. We all know that our talents are infinite. She actually did me a great service. She is a healing master'.

Shortly afterwards, Ted sat in the audience watching the first performance of his stage play. He graciously accepted the applause. 'There is a group of people who want to meet you,' the director whispered. Ted nervously ambled over to the group. 'We just loved the play,' one of them said. 'How many have you written?'

'Just one,' Ted replied.

The group looked at each other. 'That's amazing. It's as though you have been telling stories for years. What a great first attempt.'

Ted looked away embarrassed. The actress who played Marianne eased him away from the group. 'Have you thought about expanding the play into a novel? It would also make a great television series. I can make the introductions if you like.'

A publisher specialising in business management asked Ted to write a series of articles. He declined. 'What do I know about management?' he shrugged.

Ted did launch his creativity courses into the business sector. He used storytelling as an analogy to help managers find and implement their personal story-lines. He showed them how to integrate individual story-lines into the business arena to maximise business success.

Ted contracted into the business world for three months. He saw the old pattern emerging and did not seek to renew his contract. 'That was close,' he told Marianne. 'It's difficult sometimes to put old stories back on the shelf.'

Nine months after his return to Australia, he celebrated his rebirth by returning to the United Kingdom for a four-week tour. It worked! The promoter asked him to go back the following year.

He won a contract with a publisher that he had only dreamt about before. He searched his soul and wrote his story. Ted found where his heart lived. He hopes it will be a best-seller.

Ted's screen saver on his laptop computer now reads: 'For there is one alone and there is no other, and if we did but know are eternally it'. Ram Dass.

Chapter 17

Questions and Answers

Some people attend my seminars and workshops searching for answers. That's good because they are on their special quests to find the Holy Grail. It's an interesting dynamic being a seminar presenter. People attend to learn something about a common topic. In this case, it is to learn more about hands-on healing. They book their tickets and pay hard-earned money to listen to someone who they believe knows more than they do. My advertising touts that I am a Reiki and Seichim master, a psychic, intuitive, former businessman, author and so on. In other words, promoters and publicists develop pre-seminar advertising to establish the credibility of the speaker.

The upside of this is that people feel the need to come and to listen to me. Hence, ticket sales and, you guessed it, we are in business and earning a living. The downside is that people may see me as an authority on the subject. Why is this a problem? Because, if people see me in an authoritative light, then I become the Aussie serpent in the tree reinforcing their belief that they are ignorant. After all, I am a healing master, and they need me to attune them into healing mastery.

Pause for a moment and imagine reading a seminar brochure that says: 'Bruce Way will be speaking at the Royal Albert Hall in London, on Tuesday, 15 September between 7 pm and 10 pm'. Unless you know who I am and like listening to me talk, you probably would pass over the advertisement. On the other hand, if it generated a spark of interest you might call the booking office and ask for more information. Imagine that the information arrives in your mailbox. Your address is in simple type and is in a plain envelope. You open it. Take out the flier which is headed 'Further Information About the Bruce Way Seminar'. The heading on the front cover reads: 'Bruce Way will be speaking at the Royal Albert Hall in London, on Tuesday, 15 September between 7 pm and 10 pm'.

Well, you already knew that. You open the flier and on the inside printed in black ink in a standard typeface are the words, 'Come and hear what he has to say on the topic of healing'. Now, that's enlightening! At least you know the topic! You turn to the back of the brochure thinking, 'What can I learn from this man?'. Perhaps the brochure is psychic because the answer is on the back. It says: 'Bruce can't tell you anything that you don't know already. You have the answers to all your questions. You just have to remember them'.

Somehow, I don't think that I would get a huge response to the seminar. Yet, this is how I approach all my talks. I assume that all the wisdom that I need to draw on is in the audience. I assume that the seminar is a meeting of masters who have decided to come together to share energies in the form of experiences. Specifically, at my seminars I am the person talking about my experiences and the knowledge that I have gained through my particular journey. I am not a guru, an expert, or a master other than for myself. I try to make this very clear at the beginning of my talks.

Indeed, I hope that this message has come through in this book. When I talk publicly, I simply take on the role of a symbol for the audience. That is, I am just an external representation of their desires to remember that they are whole. I find it interesting that the theme that runs through letters and comments of thanks is not that I have taught some huge enlightening revelation. Rather it is that I have confirmed what the person has been thinking for some time yet hasn't been able to express effectively. This to me is the role of a storyteller. We are the ones who bring out the knowledge that is already in people so that they can see it expressed in the external world and embrace it consciously.

I remember, as a student, attending the first lecture on intelligence at Latrobe University in Melbourne. I remember how the lecturer, a short man, peered over the lectern. I remember being awe-struck as he began the lecture. I remember the authority that he showed and his poise as he presented the information. I realised just how much of a student I was, compared to this man. He could teach me so much from his wisdom. 'This course will be as exciting as you want to make it,' he began. 'For the next twelve weeks we are going to explore the nature of intelligence and by the end of the module I hope that you will have more questions than answers.'

Now that was a new twist. As psychology students, we were at university to learn and to demonstrate what we had learned by answering questions either by assignment or direct tests and examinations. 'Intelligence,' he went on, 'is socially determined. It is my thesis that there is no absolute benchmark for assessing intellect'.

This was a radical statement as, just the year before, we were versed in the administration of the Intelligence Quotient, or IQ, tests. 'Suppose we travelled into the Australian desert. There we find an Aborigine and bring him back to our IQ laboratory here on campus. We put him through the battery of IQ tests that Western academia has developed. After scoring the Aborigine's test responses I imagine that he would be ranked as primal and unintelligent.'

Sixty students sat dumbfounded. Apart from the racist overtones of his statement, how could the Aborigine even begin to answer the questions without sufficient training to do so? Someone dared to voice this concern.

'Exactly,' the lecturer declared triumphantly. 'Now let's hypothetically transport you to the Aborigine's homeland. We will dress and equip you the same as our Aboriginal friend. This means you will take off most of your protective clothing and be equipped with a boomerang, a spear and nothing much else. Then we will instruct you to survive in the desert for a month. That's the Aboriginal equivalent of our intelligence tests.' By now, we were all getting the picture. The lecturer continued, 'The only difference is that the Aborigine failing the Western IQ test would be ranked intellectually inferior and put on government subsidies.

'I suggest that you would fail the outback IQ test. In the desert, it would not be a score on a test sheet, rather we would know by seeing you either dead or alive. Now whose IQ system has more resting on the outcome?' The good professor certainly delivered his message on the point of a spear. Yet, he hadn't finished.

'My belief is that intelligence can't be measured in an academic way. Intelligence is not about providing answers to questions. Rather we can assess intelligence by the quality of questions that are asked and how relevant they are to the survival of the individual in his or her environment.' Then came the bombshell. 'Well, that is all the lecture material for this semester. To those who want to continue the course I suggest that you start asking questions.'

That is how the course developed. Each lecture and tutorial consisted solely of people asking questions about the topic, in this case exploring intelligence. The lecturer chaired the sessions and after each question, he asked the person, 'Well, what do you think the answer is?'. They would respond or ask the group to answer. Whenever they answered the question, he would reply, 'Perhaps so'. Whenever another student answered the question, he would reply to the questioner, 'What do you think about that answer?'. Then he would add: 'Just remember that someone else's answer has nothing to do with your reality. Yet, you will find the light by observing your reaction to the answers given. Do you have any questions about that?'

The lecturer's response reminded me of a Sufi story about a

court hearing. The two parties were disputing ownership of a chicken. The plaintiff put his case perfectly, to which the judge responded, 'You are right'. The defendant objected vehemently and then put his case just as succinctly. The judge responded by saying, 'Yes, you are right'. The jury observing the situation exclaimed, 'But they can't both be right'. To which the judge responded, 'That's right'.

I must confess that I take the same stance as the lecturer and the Sufi judge. This book represents a summary of my beliefs at the time that I wrote it. I have not written it to be a definitive work containing all the answers on healing. In fact, in a year's time I could well have changed my mind. It is my aim to create more questions in your mind than answers, then to inspire you to find how the answers relate to the flavour of your life and the aftertaste of your experiences. Usually, my audiences know how I am going to answer their questions: 'I don't know. What do you think?'.

How can I inspire you? I know that you are all knowledgeable. You are the creator of your life and it is your divine charter to remember that you are whole. All that I can do is to ask you to take up your bed and walk. My answers to your questions are irrelevant to you. Your answers to your questions represent the wisdom that you are. Blessings and peace.

Recommended Reading

The following titles are works that I have personally read and which have influenced my approach to healing. Naturally, there are numerous books 'out there' on the subject of healing. Some books suit some people; other books suit other people. I always suggest to my students that they let their intuition do the browsing. Mastery is also about finding out the wisdom you need for yourself, irrespective of what someone else recommends.

Directly related works

Brennan, Barbara, *Hands of Light*, Bantam, New York, 1988

Church, Dawson and Sherr, Dr Alan, *The Heart of the Healer*, Penguin, New York, 1989

Hay, Louise, *You Can Heal Your Life*, Specialist Publications, Sydney, 1988

Stein, Diane, *Essential Reiki — A Complete Guide to an Ancient Healing Art*, Crossing Press, Freedom, CA, 1995

Philosophically related works

Bach, Richard, *One*, Pan Books, London, 1989

Way, Bruce, *Living Intuitively — Reaping Life's Rich Benefits*, Lothian Books, Melbourne, 1995

—, *Psychic or Charlatan — How to Interpret a Psychic Reading*, Lothian Books, Melbourne, 1996